SOUTH
ASIA

Beyond the
Global Financial Crisis

SOUTH ASIA

Beyond the Global Financial Crisis

Edited by

Amitendu Palit

NEW JERSEY · LONDON · SINGAPORE · BEIJING · SHANGHAI · HONG KONG · TAIPEI · CHENNAI

Published by

World Scientific Publishing Co. Pte. Ltd.

5 Toh Tuck Link, Singapore 596224

USA office: 27 Warren Street, Suite 401-402, Hackensack, NJ 07601

UK office: 57 Shelton Street, Covent Garden, London WC2H 9HE

British Library Cataloguing-in-Publication Data
A catalogue record for this book is available from the British Library.

SOUTH ASIA
Beyond the Global Financial Crisis

ISBN-13 978-981-4335-25-6
ISBN-10 981-4335-25-8

Typeset by Stallion Press
Email: enquiries@stallionpress.com

Printed in Singapore.

Contents

Preface

The financial crisis of 2008 was in several ways a crisis for globalisation. The globalised modern world had not experienced a crisis of this magnitude before. The Asian meltdown of 1997 was an event which was confined to Southeast and Northeast Asia. The latest crisis, however, took on a much greater geographical shape. Although it began as a 'trans-atlantic' crisis, it soon spread rapidly to various parts of the world, including Asia. This happened on account of the substantial links that the world had developed through financial globalisation channels of trade and banking. Asia was not an exception in this regard. Thus, the crisis was largely interpreted as a catastrophe arising from the close interconnectedness of financial and commercial systems which successfully transmitted the damage from its core to the periphery.

South Asia is an unusual part of the world in terms of its patchy connectedness to the rest of the globe. Some segments of the region developed strong trade and financial linkages with other countries. But there are several countries in the region whose integration with global trade, and particularly global finance, is limited. In that sense, the region was not expected to be a major casualty of the financial crisis. However, concerns about the region and the challenges that it may face following the crisis stem from the vulnerabilities that it was already nursing. South Asia's traditional vulnerabilities have been ethnic conflicts, insurgencies, poverty, natural disasters and political instability. Domestic economic slowdown inflicted by partial setbacks experienced by trade and financial sectors on account of the financial crisis can create enabling conditions for further accentuation of the existing vulnerabilities. These issues prompted South Asia's concern about the ramifications of the crisis.

The Institute of South Asian Studies (ISAS) organises an annual international conference that brings together distinguished academics, professionals and policymakers from different parts of the world to analyse emerging prospects and challenges for the region. The 5th international conference held on 4 November 2009 was devoted to the impact of the financial crisis on the region. The emphasis of the conference, in line with the institute's emphasis on studying contemporary issues in South Asia from a multi-disciplinary perspective, focused on gathering a range of perspectives on economic, social and political implications for South Asia. This volume puts together those diverse perspectives. The authors of the papers are distinguished experts in the respective subjects they have written on.

The focus of the papers include a wide variety of issues ranging from financial implications of the global financial crisis to concerns pertaining to efficient performance of local governments, terrorism, conflict management, the role of extra-regional actors in the regional strategic matrix, and the possibility of countries cooperating for building efficient regional architectures. The papers not only analyse contemporary aspects of their respective themes, but also reflect upon futuristic perceptions. In this sense, the current collection emerges as a volume that not only documents contemporary challenges in the region, but also possible options for addressing these challenges.

Editing the volume has been an enlightening and intellectually gratifying experience. I express my sincere thanks to Professor Tan Tai Yong, Director of ISAS, for giving me the opportunity to edit the book. His guidance and advice at every step has been crucial to the successful completion of the project. The conference could not have taken place without untiring efforts of my good friend and former colleague Hernaikh Singh, the former Associate Director of ISAS. The ISAS administration led by Asha Choolani has extended all possible support to the project and I express my sincere thanks to all my administrative colleagues. My research colleagues, Sasidaran Gopalan, Suvi Dogra and Gayathri Lakshminarayan, have chipped in with spirited efforts whenever required. This entire project would not have seen the light of the day had it not been for the painstaking and tire-less efforts put in by my colleague Sithara Doriasamy at ISAS and Samantha Yong at World Scientific. My sincere thanks are also due to V Sandhya at World Scientific for initiating the project. Finally, I wish to express my sincere thanks and deep gratitude to Ambassador Gopinath Pillai, Chairman of ISAS, for his continuous support and encouragement to all research and outreach activities at ISAS.

Amitendu Palit
25 October 2010

Introduction

South Asia: Beyond the Global Financial Crisis*

K. Shanmugam

Introduction

The topic here is "South Asia: Beyond the Global Financial Crisis". Let me make two preliminary points before I set out my views.

Economic focus

The focus of the question posed is primarily economic. The unstated assumption behind the question is that the recent economic crisis was the major hurdle that had to be crossed, and the question now is: What next?

That paradigm may not fit easily with the problems currently being faced by some of the countries in South Asia. For example, in the case of Pakistan, the threats it is facing from terrorism and insurgencies are probably more pressing than the consequences of the world economic crisis. In the case of Sri Lanka, the more pertinent question is: Will the peace be won and if so how? The country, with its well-educated population and abundant resources, will move forward quickly, if the peace is managed well, the world economic crisis and its after effects notwithstanding. The reconstruction of the country alone can be a major factor in progress. Similar points can be made in respect of some of the other countries in South Asia.

---

* This is an edited transcript of the keynote address by Minister K. Shanmugam at the 5th International Conference on South Asia, 4 November 2009.

1

The question that has been posed in this conference can however be asked of India, at this point in time: it is the biggest economy in South Asia, it is plugged in relatively more to the world economy and has therefore felt more of the impact of the crisis; and while it has some very serious non-economic challenges, on the whole, its economic transformation can be expected to have some impact on the world. I will therefore speak on India.

"Beyond the crisis"

The second preliminary point I want to make is this: The title is "*Beyond* the Crisis". I do hope that the optimism in that title, at this juncture, will be borne out by events — we hope that the organisers are indeed prescient, and that we will not face the various letters that have been thrown at us: a "W" or an "L", or a very fat "U".

India: Beyond the Crisis

Now, let me turn to the topic of India, beyond the crisis. Anyone wanting to speak about India faces a challenge or an opportunity, depending on how you look at it; anything you say about India is likely to be true, however contradictory the statements. It is so vast, so varied, with people of so many different persuasions, attitudes, beliefs and talents.

This amazing mix, in the context of its geography and history, has produced extremes: of phenomenal human achievement; and at the same time, there is serious underachievement for some as well.

So you can focus on the glass being half full or it being half empty.

In this context, how should one try and understand India and its economic potential, and what it will be like after the current crisis?

Many of you are experts on India. It is therefore unnecessary for me to go into a detailed discussion of India's economic potential. Instead, I will take an outsider's perspective and consider how outsiders often perceive India. And I will touch on one of the aspects that should inform such a perspective, for a better understanding of India. Second, I will touch on how one can expect India to perform after this crisis. Third, I will also touch on India's economic engagement with this region, post-crisis.

Outsider's Perspectives of India

Observers of the Indian economy often recount some well-known facts: It is a US$1.2 trillion economy and has been growing in the recent past at between 6 to 9 percent per annum. It has an almost inexhaustible supply of labour as well as high-quality human capital. Its people are hardworking, industrious and are motivated to make a better life for themselves. English is widely spoken and there is a high premium on education. It has natural resources. It has a large domestic market including a growing middle class.

Based on these facts, it is possible to project certain straight-line economic outcomes, and people often do so. Such projections are based on the experiences of other societies.

When such projections are made they are also usually accompanied by a list of things that need to be tackled by India: infrastructure, inclusive development, education, female empowerment, urban management, environment management and so on.

These are all true. Outsiders know it. Indians know it. Most sensible people can see what is needed to fully release India's energies and harness those energies towards progress. It is not rocket science.

But these straight-line projections, assumptions based on the experience of other societies, the logical list of things to do, all of these often lead to expectations of performance. And in the case of India, there has been a discernible gap between the projections and actual performance. That gap increases or decreases at various times depending on various factors — and is usually accompanied respectively by either euphoria or extreme angst. Eventually, some throw their hands up in despair.

India's Unique Experiment

The angst and despair can be avoided, and elation tempered, if one is able to make a more realistic assessment of how India will progress.

For that, it is necessary to appreciate that India is engaged in a unique political experiment that has not been tried by any other society; and that in the abstract, a political scientist may well consider that experiment to be a near impossible one.

To explain what I mean, it is useful to contrast the Indian experiment with two other models: the Anglo-Saxon model and the East Asian Tiger model.

The Anglo-Saxon model

The UK and the US rose to great preeminence and economic strength. Their societies developed under a liberal political model.

But it is important to note some key facets of that progress: The political model was liberal, but in the early years of development, the class of people who could take part in politics was limited and largely restricted to: landed, white, male. In Britain, before the Reform Act of 1832, only 1.8 percent of adults in Britain had the vote. After that Act, 2.7 percent got the vote. After the Second Reform Act of 1884, 12.1 percent got the vote. When we talk about the development of British democracy, these facts are not usually appreciated. It was not until 1930 that Britain got universal suffrage. The US did not get universal suffrage until 1965.

Thus, in both countries, in the early years and for a long period thereafter, you had people with similar value systems, similar backgrounds and often similar economic interests who had the franchise. In this environment, there was relative stability, laws were made, there was economic growth, a middle class grew. Eventually, larger and larger sections of the population obtained the franchise. In the US, when the economic interests diverged sharply, there was a civil war.

The East Asian model

On the other hand, the East Asian model took a different path in its form: a group of men (usually men) centralised power, planned in the long-term interests of the country and executed those plans quite smoothly. Some of these countries did not hold elections.

This is not to say there were no abuses of power in some of the East Asian societies which adopted this approach. There were. But on the whole, the countries progressed. People received education, were empowered, the infrastructure developed, the economies grew steadily. And there was, as a result, tremendous progress.

The system required often huge sacrifices in the longer-term interests of the country.

I will make another point as an aside. There is no clear correlation between dictatorship and progress and I am not suggesting that there is such a correlation. Outside of East Asia, in the post-World War II period, dictatorships have in fact a poor record in delivering progress to the country as a whole — but then, the sad fact is that democracies also have a poor record in those countries.

I am no political scientist, but the common theme I find in the Anglo-Saxon model and the East Asian Tigers is this: in the early stage of economic development, the political systems were relatively stable. In the Anglo-Saxon model, stability was achieved partly by reason of the limited franchise and the inherent nature of the society; and in the East Asian model, stability was imposed — and the societies were willing to accept that.

Let us now turn to India.

India

Post-World War II, India was one of the poorer countries in the world. Literacy rates were low. The people, particularly women, were not empowered.

In that environment, India gave the franchise to its entire population: the most diverse ethnic, religious mix it is possible to imagine. Since independence, India has been working on keeping intact as a sovereign entity, and modernising itself, while engaged in this unique democratic experiment.

In the annals of human history, I do not think there has ever been such an experiment. Just consider the task: More than one billion people now. It was over 500 million in the early post-independence years. As I said earlier, a most complicated mix of ethnicities and religions, with a mixed record of social peace. Vast sections of the population economically, educationally and socially disadvantaged. The additional complications of societal hierarchics, including the caste system. Weak infrastructure. A federal structure with devolution of power to the states.

How do you manage a country like this, and with the requirement of a Parliamentary majority? That is why I said a political scientist might, in the abstract, consider such a democratic experiment, with full franchise, extremely difficult in such a society.

But India has defied all naysayers and has proved to be surprisingly resilient. Its very existence as a sovereign entity, despite all the issues it has faced, both externally and internally, is quite a feat. Indeed, reasonable observers may well question if India could have survived as a single entity if it had any other political system.

And as a result of the universal franchise, we get the amazing spectacle known as the Indian General Elections, much romanticised. It is a noble ideal that has been much celebrated.

But that romanticism and idealism should not prevent us from accepting some realities that flow inevitably from this unique experiment — you could call it the price of democracy.

What are these realities? There are many. I will mention three: When such a diverse mix of electorate has the franchise, you are going to get an equally diverse mix of legislators and parties. Many irreconcilably competing interests will find voice and jostle for power.

Second, popularity wins you elections. But those who are popular are not necessarily always those who are best able to deliver governance — particularly when electability depends on being able to champion narrow ethnic/religious causes. The lower literacy levels and level of development has meant that vast sections of the population have not always been able to identify those who are able to govern and separate them from those who can only appeal to emotion. Many will of course remember that Dr. Singh himself had difficulties getting elected.

Third, such a political system encourages a mindset of trying to get a share of existing, scarce resources for a particular community, rather than engaging with others in the broader task of increasing the resources available.

All of this imposes economic costs. But the cost is not only economic. The various other costs are well documented. India ranks 134th in the UNDP Development Index. Infant mortality is high. India has a literacy rate of 61 percent. Female literacy rate is at 48 percent. UNESCO ranks India 102nd out of 129 countries in its Education for All Development Index.

These and many other observations can be made and have been made. But as outsiders, we have to accept the system as it is, and work with it. And we have to accept that such system will mean that the list of things that most people accept needs to be done — infrastructure, education and so on — may appear to be "no brainers" but it is not easy to get them done. Indeed, it will be quite difficult to get them done, because of the unique nature of the political process.

The bottom line therefore simply is this: India is different and unique. Let us accept that it is different and unique. If we apply the yardstick of other societies, we will end up being frustrated. Make a realistic assessment of what is doable in India, given the nature of the political system. Stop prescribing, theorising and romanticising. Understand the difficulties, and accept the realities. Then, there will be no gap between expectation and actualisation. Or at least the gap will be smaller.

That is my first point, as an outsider observing India. Let me now deal with my second point, India post-crisis.

India: Post-Crisis

How will India do after this crisis? The answer is fairly straightforward. The crisis is transient, temporary. Indian growth is a permanent story. India appears to be set on a path of steady growth. It should easily register 6 to 8 percent growth. If it tweaks a few things, a 9 to 10 percent average is very doable.

The *Wall Street Journal* (3 November 2009) made the following points, in part quoting Dr. Manmohan Singh:

- India should aim for 9 to 10 percent growth, as it rebounds from the global downturn.

- India has weathered the crisis better than most countries, registering a more than 6 percent growth despite a drop in exports and a poor monsoon season.
- Now, there is a palpable sense of optimism that India is on a path to return to, or even outstrip, the 9 percent growth rates it enjoyed before the downturn.
- Corporate earnings are improving and foreign institutional investors are placing big bets on India.

There is little doubt about India's growth trajectory. It is going to be one of the stories of the first half of this century, this crisis and other economic crises notwithstanding.

There are threats to this picture. India faces a well-armed, well-trained Maoist insurgency in the Northeast which has spread to the East. This is seen as a serious threat.

India also faces terrorist threats throughout the country; and it faces threats from communalism and other similar social forces.

India's ability to deal with these threats through the exercise of political will has been hampered by the nature of its political system. But its large mass and the innate common sense and nature of the Indian people have allowed it so far to absorb the shocks.

These and other threats could cloud the economic picture. But on the whole, the sense is that India will make steady progress despite all these threats, though the rate of growth may be affected.

Now let me turn to the third of my three points: the level of economic engagement between India and this region, after this crisis.

Engagement Between India and Southeast Asia

From a Southeast Asian perspective, there are at least four major economic powers which seek to play a role in this region: the US, China, Japan and India.

The US of course has long been a partner in this region. Economically, it is a most important presence. Likewise, Japan. Both the US and Japan have had a long history of economic engagement and have very strong ties and influence in this region. They have invested billions of dollars, there are strategic engagements and they employ hundreds of thousands of people across the region.

China is a relative newcomer to this region, if we start looking at it from the post-World War II period. However, it has quickly established itself as a major player with substantial influence: ASEAN–China trade in 2008 was US$200 billion and growing. China has strong bilateral ties with many countries and gives a lot of aid and technical assistance to countries in this region. And its open approach to free trade agreements (FTAs) and other similar economic engagements has found resonance and strong support in Southeast Asia.

ASEAN and China agreed to launch negotiations for an FTA in November 2001. A Framework Agreement on Comprehensive Economic Cooperation was signed a year later. In 2005, the Agreement on Trade in Goods entered into force. The Trade in Services Agreement entered into force in 2007. In August 2009, the Investment Agreement, which is the third and final pillar of the ASEAN–China Free Trade Area, was signed. China also started a US$10 billion China–ASEAN Investment Cooperation Fund to finance investment cooperation, and plans to offer US$15 billion of commercial credit to support infrastructure development in ASEAN.

Ties with China will deepen and strengthen fairly quickly. China seems to have a clear strategy in this respect, and its strategy (as can be expected of China) is being executed well.

India has been showing increasing interest at a time when the US and Japan have established a strong presence and when China is engaged in a big way with Southeast Asia.

India launched its "Look East" policy in 1992. That policy has had a number of aspects. One is the military aspect. India has sought to play a bigger role in maritime security in this region. It has had some military engagements with some countries in this region.

On the economic front, India has engaged with ASEAN. In 2003, ASEAN and India inked a Framework Agreement to pave the way for an ASEAN–India Free Trade Area. After six years of negotiations, ASEAN and India signed the Trade in Goods Agreement in August 2009, which is the first of three substantive pillars of the FTA.

Negotiations will now have to take place on the other two substantive pillars, namely services and investments.

The negotiations on Open Skies Agreement have not been finalised. Various initiatives under the 2004 Plan of Action are pending. They may take some time. The pace of all these engagements will be dictated by what is possible between ASEAN and India.

In due course, as India grows economically, India could play a greater economic role in this region. The private sector is likely to lead the way. ASEAN is now India's third largest trading partner. ASEAN–India trade has increased 17-fold from US$2.3 billion in 1991/1992 to US$39 billion in 2007/2008. The ASEAN–India FTA envisages that trade may reach US$50 billion by 2010.

And Singapore is the most important of India's ASEAN trading partners, accounting for US$15.5 billion or 40 percent of the trade. Singapore surpassed the US and UK in 2008 to become India's largest investor, after Mauritius.

Thus, from an economic perspective, there is reason to be optimistic: India will grow; India's economic engagement, particularly private sector engagement in this region, will grow; and Singapore's role in that engagement will grow as well.

For a variety of reasons, Indian companies and business persons find Singapore an attractive place to locate to do business in the region. And we will continue to make it so. The potential is great and in this respect, there is every likelihood of the potential being realised, after this economic crisis. India holds a lot of promise for savvy investors, with emphasis on the word "savvy".

Before I end, I would like to take this opportunity to offer my heartiest congratulations to Mr. Gopinath Pillai, Ambassador-at-Large and Chairman of the Institute of South Asia Studies, on being awarded the Public Service Star (Bar) at this year's National Day Awards Ceremony. Mr. Pillai, or Gopi as he is affectionately known, has given many years of dedicated service to Singapore and the award is a fitting recognition of his invaluable services.

Thank you. I trust all of you will have a fruitful conference.

Chapter 1

South Asia and the Global Financial Crisis: Impacts and Implications

Amitendu Palit

Introduction

The outbreak of the global financial crisis in September 2008 sprang a few surprises, although there was probably not much surprise in world economic activity slowing down. A deceleration in the global economy was expected given the vulnerabilities it had developed. Foremost among these was the unrealistic high prices of property and capital assets. High prices had, as such, become pervasive in the world economy with food, oil, minerals and other commodity prices sky-rocketing. Most countries, particularly in the developing world, were struggling to tackle rising inflation that was eroding household savings.

From a broader global perspective, exchanges between economies had become increasingly unbalanced with large deficits building up in inter-country trade and capital flows. Nachane ('Global Crisis, Financial Institutions and Reforms'; Chapter 1) provides a detailed account of factors that led to the outbreak of the crisis. One of the most visible signs of the impending calamity was the stress affecting the global banking system with balance sheets of several banks in the US and Europe showing a sharp rise in liabilities due to the poor quality of assets held against loans. Large non-performing assets (NPAs) in the banking system, imbalanced trade relationships between major economies (e.g. US and China) and unusually high commodity prices were unmistakable symptoms of the global economy heading for a slowdown.

While the retardation was not entirely unexpected, what was most surprising was its intensity. The world economy ground to a major halt with world output growth dropping from 3.0 percent in 2008 to –0.6 percent in 2009.[1] The year 2009 was one of the worst years for the world economy in recent times as it experienced the brunt of the economic debacle that set in from September 2008. A decline in global economic growth was expected by many, though most did not expect it to turn negative. The bigger shock, however, came in form of the extreme turbulence experienced by the global financial system. The International Monetary Fund (IMF) has estimated total losses of the US and European banks at US$2.8 trillion during the period 2007–2010.[2] Several leading financial institutions (e.g. Bear Sterns, Lehmann Brothers, Merrill Lynch, Fannie Mae, Freddie Mac, Washington Mutual and AIG) failed during the crisis. Some of these have been subsequently taken over by respective country governments while some others have been acquired. The almost synchronised collapse of these institutions in quick succession created widespread panic in financial markets. As equity prices tumbled, investors lost large parts of their wealth. Problems were further complicated by the fact that almost all savings instruments held by households and individuals across the world were linked to financial markets. As the latter nosedived, so did the returns on personal savings, thereby reducing the financial solvencies of individuals.

The setback suffered by financial markets was accompanied by a sharp downturn in world trade. Growth in world trade declined to –11.3 percent in 2009.[3] Much of the decline was a result of exporters and importers not getting enough credit from banks for financing

---

[1] 'Restoring Confidence without Harming Recovery'; *World Economic Outlook Update*; International Monetary Fund (IMF), Washington, 7 July 2010; http://www.imf. org/external/pubs/ft/weo/2010/update/02/pdf/0710.pdf. Accessed on 27 August 2010.

[2] 'Factbox-U.S, European Bank writedowns, credit losses'; http://www.reuters.com/ article/idCNL554155620091105?rpc=44. Accessed on 27 August 2010.

[3] See Footnote 1.

their shipments. Banks had become over-cautious in lending for obvious reasons. The world trade community bore the brunt of their cautiousness. Along with trade, there was also a decline in global investments, which was expected. For several developing countries, a serious concern was the decline in remittances from workers settled abroad.

More Financial, Less Economic

As the crisis matured and the world reconciled to one of the worst episodes of economic downturn since the Great Depression of the 1930s, a few aspects of the crisis became distinct. There was sharp variation in the intensity of the crisis among different regions of the world. The West was hit far worse than the East. The US and Europe suffered most from setbacks in financial institutions and markets. The largest number of bankruptcies occurred in the US and Europe. In contrast, the intensity of the damage was less in Asia. Within Asia as well, differences were visible in the degree of its impact on different economies. East and Southeast Asia were worse affected than South and Central Asia. Within East and Southeast Asia, Japan, Korea, Taiwan, Hong Kong and Singapore were more affected than China, Indonesia, the Philippines and Vietnam. In South Asia, India, the largest economy of the region was more affected than the others.

It also became increasingly clear that the crisis was more a 'financial' catastrophe than an 'economic' one. Financial markets crashed; global trade also decelerated sharply. But even then, there were hardly any instances of countries plunging into external debt crises or defaulting on their existing payment obligations. Very few countries approached the IMF for assistance in bailing them out. It was actually 'financial' globalisation, entailing close connection between financial markets, institutions (e.g. banks, hedge funds) and instruments (e.g. mutual funds, insurance and pension plans) that faced its worst crisis, rather than 'economic' globalisation, which envisages integration of not only financial markets, but also others such as commodities, labour, technology and knowledge. In this sense, the crisis was more aptly a 'financial' crisis, rather than an 'economic' crisis. This is, of course, not to suggest that the two are entirely exclusive of each other. Financial crisis creates considerable economic damage as it did during its current manifestation. However, other certain aspects of economic systems and transactions were relatively less-affected. Indeed, post-facto analysis in the distant future might interpret the crisis as purely a banking sector calamity confined to the US and Europe.

Financial markets were the main channel through which the 'trans-Atlantic' crisis travelled to Asia. Trade was the other route through which Asian economies were affected. Asian countries with developed financial markets and closely integrated with Western financial institutions such as Hong Kong, Japan, Korea, Taiwan and Singapore were the most affected. Their plights became worse because of their additional dependence on external trade. In contrast, countries like China and India, despite not escaping the crisis, were relatively less troubled. The most important reason for this was the relative under-exposure of their banks and financial institutions to those in the West. The primarily government-owned banking systems in both countries hardly had any connections with failed financial institutions in the West. As a result, banking systems in both countries continued to function normally. However, both countries were hit by the deceleration in global trade. As the crisis reduced purchasing powers and appetite for Asian exports in the West, trade contracted sharply with inventories of unsold products building up in both China and India. While India experienced the financial crisis through the 'trade', and not the 'financial' channel, the rest of South Asia was even less affected. Trade declined for all other major economies of the region such as Pakistan, Bangladesh and Sri Lanka. The damages, however, were confined to a few specific export-oriented sectors such as readymade garments and textiles. Given that external trade contributes much less to these economies compared with those in East and Southeast Asia, the magnitude of the economic setback was also proportionally less. Furthermore, complete insulation from failed banks in the West helped in protecting the domestic financial sectors as well.

Crisis and South Asia: Connections and Concerns

South Asia's concerns with the crisis extended far beyond its domain of immediate economic impact. Being one of the relatively less globalised parts of the world, South Asian economies are not fully synchronised with cycles characterising major world economies. As a result, the economic downturn did not assume as grave proportions in South Asia as it did elsewhere in the world. Concerns in South Asia focused on whether the economic slowdown, despite being relatively less calamitous, will aggravate existing vulnerabilities in the region. As Minister Shanmugam mentions, problems of terrorism and insurgency in South Asia have origins and consequences different from those of the global financial crisis ('South Asia: Beyond the Global Financial Crisis'; Introduction). Similarly, South Asia's chronic vulnerabilities of poor governance, high poverty, deficient infrastructure, low literacy, malnutrition, susceptibility to natural disasters, political instability and ethnic conflicts perpetuate due to complex combinations of diverse economic, social and political factors. None of these are directly connected to a financial catastrophe of trans-Atlantic origin. Nonetheless, situations of economic downturn often act as catalysts for exacerbating downsides of existing problems.

Episodes of low economic growth and less economic activity imply a slower expansion of opportunities. As businesses become reluctant to expand, investments reduce and cost-cutting gather momentum, the retrenchment of existing workers is accompanied by freezes on new recruits. In low-income countries with surplus workers, such as those in South Asia, contracting labour markets often trigger widespread economic and political unrests. The latter can reinforce those that are already prevailing due to conflicts. Quick economic recoveries do not necessarily improve situations fast. Labour market indicators like employment usually lag behind economic indicators like GDP (Gross Domestic Product) growth. Even if GDP growth stages a turnaround, employment takes time to respond positively, as businesses are slow in recovering risk-taking appetites. In Indonesia and the Philippines, unemployment has not yet reduced to pre-Asian financial crisis levels for several years despite economic growth picking up well. Similar evidence of employment responding with considerable lag is available from Korea and Thailand.[4]

Apprehensions over economic downturns accentuating socio-political vulnerabilities are particularly strong in South Asia, given the region's inability to make economic progress an 'inclusive' process. The World Bank estimates that almost half of the world's poor to live in South Asia.[5] Aiyar points out that governments in India and many other parts of the region assume injection of greater financial resources in anti-poverty programmes as the most effective way of tackling poverty ('Socio-Economic Developments in South Asia: Issues and Outlook'; Chapter 2). Increasing expenditure without efficient governance can hardly be expected to deliver desired results. South Asia is no exception in this regard. As Aiyar argues, notwithstanding landmark constitutional amendments institutionalising local self-governments in India, the poor are yet to be socially and politically empowered due to patchy governance, particularly in ensuring access to education and health. Inclusive growth will continue to remain elusive without inclusive governance. Furthermore, in situations where adverse consequences of poor governance are coupled with depressed economic conditions, the resultant outcomes may imply considerable socio-political distress.

It is, however, not easy to find solutions to these problems. From an Indian perspective, as Minister Shanmugam points out, popularity may win elections but the popular are not necessarily the best equipped to govern, given that elections are often won on narrow ethnic or religious causes. He asserts that the inability to identify capable administrators has much to do with low literacy levels and

---

[4] MacIntyre A., Pempel T.J. and Ravenhill, J (2008), 'East Asia in the Wake of the Financial Crisis' in *Crisis as Catalyst*, MacIntyre, Pempel and Ravenhill (eds.), Cornell University Press, USA; Chapter 1.

[5] More than 1 billion people in South Asia earn less than US$2 per day, which is the poverty line criteria currently adopted by the World Bank. See 'South Asia — Regional Strategy Update 2010', World Bank; http://web.worldbank.org/WBSITE/EXTERNAL/COUNTRIES/SOUTHASIAEXT/0,contentMDK:21265405~menuPK:2298227~pagePK:146736~piPK:146830~theSitePK:223547,00.html. Accessed on 28 August 2010.

under-development. This reinforces Aiyar's arguments regarding the importance of empowering the poor. However, such empowerment presupposes some semblance of good governance courtesy election of enlightened representatives by people. The desired virtuous cycle of enlightened legislators aiding empowerment of the poor, and the empowered in turn electing capable governors, may find it difficult to take off since both election and empowerment are a closely inter-related phenomenon.

The financial crisis occurred at a time when South Asia was in the throes of significant political transformations. As Aziz notes ('Political Developments in South Asia: Issues and Outlook'; Chapter 4), 2008 and 2009 were years when democracy recorded comebacks in several parts of the region. Pakistan had a democratically elected government in February 2008 after almost a decade of military rule. Bangladesh held elections in January 2009 following a two-year rule by a care-taker government. Nepal moved beyond a protracted period of civil strife to have a new Constituent Assembly in May 2008. India also held its general elections in May 2009. In Sri Lanka, the prolonged ethnic conflict and hostilities between the military and Tamil insur-gents finally ended in May 2009. Periods of political transformations are always sensitive as governments are new in assessing challenges, and political and administrative authorities of incumbent regimes are yet to be firmly established. Transformations can be even more deli-cate in those parts of South Asia where democratic foundations are on shaky grounds. In this respect, the financial crisis actually occurred at a time when South Asia would have wanted it the least.

From the vantage point of new political establishments in the region, the crisis demanded careful management of vulnerabilities. The incumbent government in India led by Prime Minister Manmohan Singh contested elections in the backdrop of lower economic growth, cutback in employment prospects and enhanced tensions with Pakistan following terrorist attacks in Mumbai in November 2008. More than the larger dimensions of the financial crisis, a critical worry for the government as it went into elections were the high prices in the economy. High food and commodity prices have significant political downsides. Along with India, governments in Pakistan and Bangladesh were also under pressure to keep prices at moderate levels. High prices in all these countries were combinations of internal deficiencies (e.g. supply shortages, poor procurement systems, inadequate storage capacities) and global developments. For electorates and domestic constituencies, however, results are more important than explanations. Responses to high prices ranged from domestic market-based measures such as the release of fresh food stocks (India, Bangladesh, Nepal and Pakistan), price control and action against hoarding (Bangladesh, Sri Lanka, Pakistan), to trade policy measures like reducing tariffs on the import of food and prohibiting food exports (Bangladesh, Pakistan, India, and Nepal).[6] India also increased allocations under, and coverage of, its National Rural Employment Guarantee Scheme (NREGS). Unfortunately, in the presence of systemic inefficiencies, these measures act with lags as far as their eventual impact and success in moderating prices are concerned. While no major political upheavals have taken place in South Asia since the crisis, high food prices remain critical concerns and political flashpoints all across the region.

Crisis and Conflict: The South Asian Scenario

Ethnic conflicts resulting in the loss of human lives and material resources have been integral features of South Asia. The relationship between poverty and income inequality and conflict has been a widely researched subject. Most of the world's conflict-prone zones, including South Asia, are low-income countries characterised by widespread poverty and income inequality. Indeed, the 'poverty-conflict trap' has become a much debated concept in modern development discourse.[7]

---

[6] *Country Responses to the Food Security Crisis : Nature and Preliminary Implications of the Policies Pursued;* Food and Agriculture Organization (FAO), United Nations; http://www.fao.org/fileadmin/user_upload/ISFP/pdf_for_site_Country_Response_to_the_Food_Security.pdf. Accessed on 28 August 2010.

[7] Poverty undermines prospects for peace and armed conflict reduces prospects for development. See Collier, P.; Lance E.; Håvard H.; Hoeffler A.; Reynal-Querol M. and Sambanis N. (2003) *Breakingthe Conflict Trap: Civil War and Development Policy,* Oxford: Oxford University Press and World Bank.

Without deliberating on the discourse, one can presume that South Asia will be an important part of the debate, given its pervasive under-development and vulnerability to armed conflicts. Matters in South Asia have probably worsened due to active 'interference' of other major global powers in regional affairs. Paul argues that geo-strategic regions with multiple weak states are ripe for activism by major powers ('The Major Powers and Conflicts in South Asia; Chapter 5). South Asia fits the bill snugly in this regard. Afghanistan is a pertinent example of a geo-strategically significant yet weak state characterised by under-development and armed conflict. It is also a country where global and regional powers of the world have been displaying active interest. Though direct causalities are difficult to establish, such activism might have aggravated conflicts in a situation where poverty and under-development are, as it is, abetting their prolongation. As Aziz points out, South Asia must make efforts to minimise adverse effects of 'global fault lines'. Needless to say, financial crises depressing growth performances and prospects are unlikely to provide for any source of optimism in these contexts. On the contrary, the off-shoot of crises in the form of high commodity prices and low trade growth are likely to complicate matters further.

There is little doubt that the perpetuation of conflict-driven vulnerabilities in South Asia has much to do with the region's inability to provide clean and efficient administrations. Discussing the growth of religious extremism in Pakistan, Rais underscores the disenchantment of common people with the present class of political leaders in providing effective and honest governments ('Religious Extremism and Terrorism in Pakistan: Chapter 6). Such disappointment is usually exploited by religious extremist organisations for projecting themselves as more endearing alternatives. The calamitous floods in Pakistan in August 2010 and the slow response of the government in rehabilitating the displaced are the latest examples where fundamental organisations exploited the delay by providing relief measures and earning "brownie points". The inability of governments to timely address consequences of financial crisis such as high commodity prices and contraction in employment opportunities display the former in a poor light. It is evident that poor governance has not only limited empowerment for the poor, as mentioned earlier, but has also provided enabling conditions for the growth of insurgency and religious extremism. India's Maoist insurgency which probably symbolises the biggest threat facing the country today is an outcome of years and decades of poor governance and economic exploitation of local communities.

Governance assumes an equally important role in maintaining peace in situations where outstanding conflicts have been resolved. Sri Lanka's economic potential has remained unexploited on account of the long ethnic conflict the country has suffered from. An end to the hostilities, Jayatilleka argues, offers a historic opportunity for embracing political reconciliation between ethnic communities ('Prospects for Conflict Resolutions in South Asia'; Chapter 7). Delays in doing so might amount to losing the rare prospect. Notwithstanding political initiatives, governance (or, more precisely, the lack of it) can minimise the peace dividend on occasions when peace has been a hard-fought achievement. Indeed, positive initiatives such as the one proposed by Chowdhury — a trilateral grouping of India, Pakistan and Bangladesh based on commonalities and aiming to solve problems rather than avoiding them ('India, Pakistan and Bangladesh: 'Trilateralism' in South Asia?'; Chapter 8) — might be a non-starter due to governance impediments.

Beyond the Crisis

The world has recovered from the financial crisis much faster than what was initially anticipated. Global output growth shrunk from 3.0 percent in 2008 to –0.6 percent in 2009. The current projections by the IMF forecast the world economy to grow by 4.6 percent and 4.3 percent respectively in 2010 and 2011.[8] Though the US and Europe continue to have depressed economic prospects, Asia, led by China and India, is spearheading the global recovery. Buoyant growth prospects for India imply similar prospects for South Asia as well. South Asia is expected to grow at a robust rate of 7.5 percent in 2010,

---

[8] See Footnote 1.

on account of strong growth in India supported by healthy economic recovery in Sri Lanka and Bangladesh.[9] The temporary deceleration inflicted by the financial crisis has obviously not lasted long in the region. Concerns, however, remain over Pakistan which has been affected by one of its worst natural disasters.

The post-financial crisis world economy is expected to be dominated by economic momentum emanating from Asia. South Asia is likely to be a major source of such momentum, along with East and Southeast Asia. The region's potential to chart and maintain an upward economic trajectory depends significantly on its success in managing internal weaknesses. The financial crisis has not left an indelible economic impact on the region. But what it has certainly done is to draw attention to where the region needs to focus on.

Political instability, armed conflict and religious extremism continue to remain significant threats to the region's economic prosperity, peace and harmony. The inspiration drawn by these threats from poverty and deprivation are clearly visible. The region is fortunate in the financial crisis not aggravating vulnerabilities further in this respect. Relatively less exposure to global financial markets and institutions was probably the main reason behind South Asia's good fortune. However, future episodes of global economic downturns might prove more injurious as the region integrates deeper into the world economy. In this respect, South Asia would do well to note that the injuries may not remain confined to economic prospects alone. Unless it is able to take significant strides in curbing its pervasive underdevelopment, the world's most populous region might experience vicious outcomes on future occasions of economic setbacks.

It is sad to note that both South Asia's problems and solutions are common knowledge. Unfortunately, despite such knowledge, efforts to eradicate problems are hardly producing the desired results. Governance is a critical gap and needs to be addressed upfront. The question concerns why it is not being addressed despite the crying

---

[9] 'Developing Asia's Recovery Gains Momentum'; *Special Note*, Asian Development Bank (ADB), Manila, July 2010; http://www.adb.org/Documents/Books/ADO/ 2010/ado-special-note-2010.pdf. Accessed on 29 August 2010.

need. Is it a problem of political unwillingness? Is it an issue of South Asian states not being strong enough to take hard decisions on governance? Or is it because South Asia's influential political and economic elites are happy with the current state of affairs and wish to preserve them for consolidating self-interests? The answer might be a combination of all these and many more unaddressed questions. Whatever it may be, there is little doubt that South Asia is nursing two equally powerful potential futures. The first is becoming an economic powerhouse. The second is degenerating into a hub of strife and squalor. The region needs to act decisively and move towards sympathetic and effective governance to ensure that the first future does not become suppressed by the second.

Chapter 2

Global Crisis, Financial Institutions and Reforms: An EME Perspective

Dilip M. Nachane

Introduction

The relationship between finance and economic growth has witnessed a lively controversy and sharp divisions among schools of economic thought. First, there are those who regard financial development as a critical precondition for economic growth (e.g. Goldsmith, 1969; Hicks, 1969; Schumpeter, 1912; etc.). Second, an influential group of economists (e.g. Seers, 1983; Lucas, 1988) believes that the role of financial institutions is incidental to economic development and hugely "over stressed" in the conventional literature, while a third group sees finance as passively adapting to developments in the real sector (most notably Joan Robinson, 1952).[1]

In recent years, there has been a marked shift in attitude towards financial development among economic growth theorists. The earlier skepticism has given way to a growing realisation that financial markets and institutions play a defining role in the economic evolution of societies. Empirical evidence based on both cross-country as well as micro-level studies lends support to the view that financial development crucially affects the speed and pattern of economic development. This it does both by influencing the composition and pace of capital accumulation as well as by promoting technological innovation.

---

[1] Several well-known tracts on development economics frequently make no reference to the financial system at all (see Meier and Seers, 1984; Stern, 1989; etc.).

The financial system is traditionally viewed as performing the following five functions (see Levine, 1997; Archer, 2006; etc.):

1. Resource allocation;
2. Mobilisation of savings;
3. Expanding goods and services markets;
4. Facilitation of risk pooling, hedging and diversification;
5. Monitoring managers and exercising corporate control.

To this list one must append an extra function, which has assumed a great deal of importance in recent years in EMEs, viz.

6. Provision of credit to the informal sector (rural as well as urban) via microfinance institutions.

However even within the broad consensus recognising the role of financial systems for economic development, important areas of disagreement persist, viz. the type of financial system most conducive to growth, private versus public ownership of financial institutions, the degree of regulation and supervision, the role of financial innovations and the pace and extent of financial liberalisation. The Latin American crises of the 1980s and 1990s, the Asian financial crisis and the current global recession have once again brought the critical role of financial institutions under the scanner, and introduced some important caveats to the consensus. The present paper aims to take stock of some of these issues in the Indian context. While it is certainly not being claimed that the Indian experience is representative of the entire South Asian region, it is nevertheless felt that some of the lessons drawn here would have some relevance transcending their immediate context.

Indian Financial System

The financial system in India comprises of the Reserve Bank of India (RBI) at the apex, numerous financial intermediaries, money market, debt market, foreign exchange market and equity market.

Financial intermediaries include commercial banks, co-operative banks and non-bank financial institutions (NBFIs). Commercial banks constitute the largest segment of India's financial system and a characteristic feature of this sector is the dominance of the public sector (PCBs) both in terms of branch offices and banking operations. Other types of banks include regional rural banks, local area banks and co-operative banks. Co-operative banking is also an integral component of India's banking system. It comprises of two major segments, viz. urban co-operative banks (UCBs) and rural co-operative credit institutions (RCCIs). Of these, RCCIs have a far more extensive branch network and a more diverse and complex structure than UCBs that maintain a single-tier structure. NBFIs are an important segment of India's financial system, embracing a heterogeneous group of diverse institutions including development finance institutions (DFIs), insurance companies, non-bank financial companies (NBFCs), primary dealers (PDs) and capital market intermediaries such as mutual funds. NBFIs offer a variety of products and services and play an important role in providing access to financial services to a vast section of the population. Recent years have also witnessed a phenomenal growth in the number of microfinance institutions (MFIs).[2]

The RBI plays an instrumental role in the Indian financial sector. Being the country's monetary authority, it formulates, implements, and monitors India's monetary policy. As a prime regulator and supervisor of India's financial system, it uses and prescribes broad parameters of banking operations within which the country's banking and financial system functions. The RBI supervises, among others, commercial banks, co-operative banks, development finance institutions (DFIs) and non-banking financial companies (NBFCs). Through its monetary policy, it aims to secure stability in the internal and external value of the Indian currency and manages the foreign exchange market. It is also the banker to the government. It provides merchant banking services to both the central and state governments.

---

[2] My forthcoming paper with Shahidul Islam of ISAS provides a comprehensive description of the financial system in the South Asian region.

The RBI also does other traditional central banking activities such as currency issuance, promotional functions, etc.

Till the early 1990s, the Indian financial system was characterised *inter alia* by administered interest rates guided by the social concerns, high intermediation costs, a low base of capital, directed credit programmes for the priority sectors, high degree of non-performing assets, low intensity of technologies, stringent entry barriers for new entrants and excessive regulations. Since the early 1990s, financial sector reforms have been initiated with the explicit objectives of developing a market-oriented, competitive, well-diversified and transparent financial system. In broad terms the reforms have addressed the following six areas: (i) removing the restrictions on pricing of assets; (ii) building of institutional and technological infrastructure; (iii) strengthening risk management practices; (iv) fine-tuning of the market microstructure; (v) changes in the legal framework to remove structural rigidities; and (vi) widening and deepening of the market with new participants and instruments. (For an extended review and critique of this process kindly refer to Nachane and Islam, 2009.)

With a view to providing some perspectives on the evolution of the financial sector in India, we present below a few basic indicators. Our first indicator is the size of the financial system (Table 1), defined as

$$S = \frac{[CBA + MC + B]}{GNP \text{ at market prices}}$$

where *CBA* is the commercial banks' assets, *MC* is the equity market capitalization and *B* is the bonds outstanding.

Table 1.   Size of the Indian Financial System

Year	CBA (Rs. Trillion)	MC (Rs. Trillion)	B (Rs. Trillion)	Total Financial Assets (Rs. Trillion)	S
March 2000	8.1687	19.3327	5.2091	32.7104	1.69
March 2005	19.1143	32.8401	12.6841	64.6384	2.07
March 2008	34.3756	99.9614	22.3368	156.6737	3.33

Financial systems differ according to the primacy of the sources of corporate finance, i.e., whether firms are financed mainly through capital markets (as in the US) or through bank loans (as in Germany). To get an idea of the relative composition of alternative sources of funding, we present two alternative indicators, viz.

$$F_1 = \frac{CBA}{MC} \quad \text{and} \quad F_2 = \frac{CBA}{(MC + B)}.$$

Tables 2 and 3 present these indicators for India over the last decade. For comparison, indicators are also presented for a few other countries.

Another important characteristic of any financial system is the ownership pattern of bank assets, i.e. the percentage of bank assets that are state-owned. For this we define a ratio

$$O_1 = \frac{\text{Assets of Public Sector Banks}}{\text{Total Bank Assets}}.$$

Table 2. Composition of the Indian Financial System: F_1

Date	India	US	UK	Germany	Japan	Korea	China
March 2000	0.4225	0.377244	0.722975	7.128747	0.025747	2.97648	3.19797
March 2005	0.5820	0.487954	0.946397	8.161254	0.017327	1.15719	5.248572
March 2008	0.3439	0.949475	2.298705	10.23022	0.026746	2.193102	2.503276

Table 3. Composition of the Indian Financial System: F_2

Date	India	US	UK	Germany	Japan	Korea	China
March 2000	0.3328	0.197723	0.541355	2.993587	0.008826	0.875696	2.492968
March 2005	0.4199	0.22998	0.673839	2.866789	0.006009	0.558997	2.800088
March 2008	0.2811	0.308487	1.215864	2.792327	0.006415	0.688694	1.492713

Table 4.   Ownership and Concentration Pattern of Indian Financial System

Date	O_1	O_2	C_B	C_E
March 2000	0.8023	0.0746	0.3969	0.3076
March 2005	0.5122	0.0443	0.2768	0.1463
March 2008	0.6990	0.0840	0.3884	0.2815

It is also of interest to define another indicator of ownership, viz. the percentage of total bank assets that are owned by foreign banks. This is given by the ratio

$$O_2 = \frac{\text{Assets of Foreign Banks}}{\text{Total Bank Assets}}.$$

One final consideration in assessing any country's financial system is the extent of its concentration. For this two indices are usually employed, viz. the share of the top five commercial banks (private or public) in total bank assets (C_s) and the share of the top five listed companies in total market equity capitalisation (C_E). The ownership and concentration statistics are presented in Table 4 (the last column representing total market equity capitalisation, C_E shows the share of the top five listed companies on the two prominent stock exchanges of India, viz. the BSE and NSE.

Global Crisis: Triggering and Aggravating Factors

The global financial crisis which took the US and much of the rest of the world by storm in late 2007 has led to a wide-ranging re-assessment of the entire gamut of issues bearing on the financial systems of advanced capitalist economies. Detailed post-mortems of the crisis (see e.g. Brunnermeier, 2009) distribute the blame in more or less equal measure among the following four causal factors:

- Great Moderation — A generic term used to describe the global situation from the 1990s onwards characterised by (i) low inflation and correspondingly low short-term interest rates, (ii) steady growth rates in the US and the Eurozone, (iii) high growth in EMEs (China and India in particular) and (iv) rising house prices across the globe.

- Global Savings Glut — This refers to several simultaneous (and mutually correlated) phenomena, viz. (i) rise in savings rates in China, Japan, OPEC and East Asia, (ii) a matching decline in savings and huge current account deficits in the US and the Eurozone, (iii) flow of global investment into US Treasury securities leading to (iv) low real long-term interest rates in the US and a correspondingly high demand for credit.

- Lax Monetary Policy — It is now generally agreed that the Greenspan years were characterised by an unwarranted easing of monetary policy in response to the dotcom bubble of 2000–01. First, there was the aggressive cutting of short-term interest rates in 2000 and 2001 and this was followed by a regime of loose monetary policy[3] over the entire period of 2001–04 leading to the home price bubble.

- Home Price Bubble — The unprecedented house price boom over 1996–2005 in the US and worldwide was sustained partly by the lax monetary policy of the US Federal Reserve (and other OECD central banks) over 2001–04 and partly by a belief that housing prices would continue their one-way movement riding on the global growth story. The phenomenal growth of subprime mortgages (covering borrowers with poor credit history and scores) especially over the period 2002–06 (when they rose from $160 bn to $600 bn) fed this bubble almost till it burst in September 2007.

From a historical perspective, the above pattern might look very similar to several past recessionary episodes but there were several new factors which sharply enhanced the magnitude of the crisis fall-out (see Ashcraft and Schuermann, 2008; Gorton, 2008; Claessens, 2009, etc.).

---

[3] The policy was loose also in a more formal way — policy rates were consistently below those predicted by various Taylor-type rules.

The first of these factors was *increased opaqueness* of the financial system brought about by complex financial instruments such as mortgage backed securities (MBS), collateralised debt obligations (CDOs) and so on. The process of securitisation spread particularly rapidly during the period 2000–07.[4] The second factor was *financial integration and interlocking* brought about by capital account openness, international financial harmonisation and the increasing presence of foreign intermediaries in several banking systems. This factor accentuated the transmission of financial shocks across borders. The final factor was the *high degree of leveraging* of financial institutions either directly through the commercial banking system (as in Europe) or through the shadow banking system[5] (as in the US). The combination of these factors resulted in a crisis of unmitigated proportions, necessitating huge bail-out and stimulus packages and resulting in huge welfare losses.

Global Crisis: Reassessment of Financial Systems

Given the scale, extent and severity of the current crisis, it is perhaps inevitable that several established theories would be challenged and several entrenched notions reviewed. The intellectual underpinnings of the advocacy of financial sector reforms in LDCs and EMEs by multilateral institutions and the developed world generally are rooted

---

[4] For example, securitisation of non-conforming mortgages (i.e. Alt-A and subprime) increased from 35 percent in 2000 to 70 percent in 2007.

[5] Shadow banking institutions are typically intermediaries between investors and borrowers. For example, an institutional investor like a pension fund may be willing to lend money, while a corporation may be searching for funds to borrow. The shadow banking institution will channel funds from the investor(s) to the corporation, profiting either from fees or from the difference in interest rates between what it pays the investor(s) and what it receives from the borrower. By definition, shadow institutions do not accept deposits like a depository bank and therefore are not subject to the same regulations. Familiar examples of shadow institutions included Bear Stearns and Lehman Brothers. Other complex legal entities comprising the system include hedge funds, SIVs, conduits, money funds, monolines, investment banks, and other nonbank financial institutions.

in two inter-related economic theories, viz. (i) the efficient markets doctrine and (ii) the McKinnon-Shaw thesis.

Efficient markets hypothesis EMH

As is well known, this hypothesis is very much in the Chicago School tradition (or what is now increasingly termed as the *freshwater* view). It posits that current market prices of financial assets embody rationally all the known information about prospective returns from the asset. Future uncertainty is of the "white noise" kind and "noise traders" (speculators) may succeed in pushing the markets temporarily away from equilibrium. But with market clearing continuously, "rational traders" will bring the system back to equilibrium, by taking counter-vailing positions and imposing heavy losses on those speculators who bet against the fundamentals. Equilibrium asset prices will therefore be altered only when there are "shocks" to the fundamentals, and while supply shocks are inevitable, the severity of demand shocks can be tempered by policy aimed at giving more access to information about fundamentals to market participants, and avoiding "policy surprises" or attempts to control asset prices. This approach has been the basis of virtually all past responses to financial crises — a response which was fundamentally skewed in that international financial institutions that usually precipitated such crises by their indiscriminate lending, rolling over of credit and tax avoidance strategies were seen in the role of victims, whereas the major blame was apportioned to the crisis-affected countries for their bungled macroeconomic management (current account deficits, overvalued exchange rates, loose monetary policy, etc.) and for "misleading" investors by withholding key information about fundamentals. Such governments were then administered bail-out packages with strong conditionalities attached as part of the IMF's "tough love" treatment.

The inappropriateness of the EMH as a description of actual trading strategies of forex traders has always been strongly suspected. Behavioural theories of human decision making (see Kahneman and Tversky, 1984; Rabin and Thaler, 2001; etc.) argue that in the face of complex uncertain situations, individuals do not proceed via maximising expected utility but by using *cognitive heuristics*. Such heuristics is an aid to reducing a complex task to a manageable proportion but often introduces systematic biases. The bulk of the econometric evidence on financial markets is also *contra* the EMH. (See e.g. Shiller, 1981, LeRoy and Porter, 1981; Shleifer and Summer, 1990; etc.).[6]

In the wake of the current crisis, economists are increasingly turning to the so-called *saltwater* view, which is essentially a resurrection of the 1930s Keynesian description of financial markets as "casinos" guided by "herd instincts" (see the public utterances of highly regarded economists such as Buiter, 2009; De Long, 2009; Krugman, 2009; etc.) In the Keynesian view, investors in financial assets are not interested in a long-term perspective, but rather in speculating on short-run price behaviour. Far from basing their expectations on prospective behaviour of the underlying fundamentals, such investors are more likely to base their opinions on market sentiments (i.e. the opinion of the other members of their group). This lends a dangerous edge of volatility to financial markets as any "news" that affects market sentiment strongly (in either direction) is likely to produce mood swings in market sentiment, even if the "news" in question is unlikely to alter long-term fundamentals.

McKinnon-Shaw thesis

This thesis essentially views financial liberalisation as an integral component of overall liberalisation, in the twin beliefs that (i) liberalisation in the real sector cannot proceed satisfactorily in the absence of financial liberalisation and (ii) financial liberalisation is an "enabling condition" of faster economic growth, as it increases competition, transfer of know-how, and transparency.

The McKinnon-Shaw case for financial liberalisation was based on the perception that *financial repression* (arising as a consequence of government control over important parameters of bank behaviour)

---

[6] Long before the current crisis, Warren Buffet once famously remarked, "I'd be a bum in the street with a tin cup if the markets were efficient".

tended to result in low (and often negative) real interest rates and an excess demand for credit. The resultant credit rationing led to credit allocation to favoured sectors by administrative fiat rather than through the purview of a market mechanism. Following financial liberalisation, real interest rates would rise to their natural levels and economic growth would result from an increased quantum of domestic savings and a rise in total factor productivity (TFP) due to an improvement in the quality of bank credit for investment purposes. As we have already noted by and large financial liberalisation does seem to promote growth in the long run. But the short-and medium-term consequences may not always be benign. Several authors have underscored the likely harmful effects of financial liberalisation in triggering financial crises and in misdirecting the allocation of capital (see Saidane, 2002; Eichengreen, 2001; etc.). Demirguc-Kunt and Detragiache (1998), for example, argue that financial liberalisation intensifies competition among banks, who in their eagerness to preserve market shares could indulge in indiscriminate and risky credit operations (moral hazard problem). During bullish periods, debt leveraging can augment the expected return from financial position-taking by corporate borrowers. Wider asset price movements also erode the ability of banks and other financial institutions to adequately collateralise their loans, while competition restrains them from raising the risk premia on loans.

Recent studies such as those by Rodrik *et al.* (2002), Alcala and Ciccone (2004) and Kaufmann *et al.* (2007) clearly indicate the importance of institutional features such as corruption, rule of law and general governance issues (such as political accountability, quality of bureaucracy, etc.) in determining whether the outcomes of financial liberalisation would be beneficial or otherwise. This could be an important part of the explanation as to why liberalisation usually succeeds in the developed countries but often fails in the developing world. It also throws up in retrospect the fallacy implicit in the reform advocacy of the 1990s which urged developing countries with weak institutions to undertake economic reforms, under the implicit assurance that political progress and good governance would follow as a consequence.

Global Crisis: Coordinated Policy Response

One distinctive feature of the current crisis is that for possibly the first time since the abandonment of the gold standard, there has been an almost instinctive recognition by policymakers globally of the need for a coordinated approach to the crisis.[7] In the early stages of the crisis, the coordination efforts were confined mainly to the G5 countries (France, UK, US, Germany and Japan) and covered three major areas, viz. liquidity provision by central banks, fiscal stimulus and the cleansing of bank balance sheets.

Thus, to begin with there was an unprecedented coordinated cut in policy rates by six major central banks in October 2008 — by 50 basis points. Second, on the liquidity provision front, the Federal Reserve authorised temporary foreign exchange swap lines with 14 different monetary authorities.[8] This unique arrangement was designed to alleviate the global shortage of dollar funding.

On the fiscal stimulus, let me quote from a recent speech[9] by the Managing Director of the IMF:

> Fiscal stimulus is less effective in more open economies, as some of the spending feeds through to imports, benefiting output and

---

[7] This is not to deny that in the immediate wake of the crisis individual country policies tended to be insular, with countries acting in an uncoordinated manner to expand lender of last resort facilities, increase protection of creditors and depositors, and recapitalise banks with public funds. This lack of coordination had some destabilising effects, at least in the short term. Two cases in particular stand out, viz. the Lehman bankruptcy and the collapse of the Icelandic banking system. When Lehman fell, countries moved immediately to ring-fence assets in their own jurisdictions. The case of Iceland was similar. Although Icelandic banks had a large number of nonresident depositors, the authorities failed to coordinate with the countries in question. Some of these countries ended up seizing Icelandic bank assets to protect their own depositors.

[8] Today, the central banks in the United Kingdom, the euro area, Switzerland and Japan all have access to unlimited swap lines across different maturities.

[9] See "Crisis Management and Policy Coordination: Do We Need a New Global Framework?", speech by Dominique Strauss-Kahn made at Oesterreichische Nationalbank, Vienna, on 15 May 2009.

employment in other countries. This is why collective action is so important, why countries must act in unison. If more countries act, the burden on each individual country is lessened.

It happened. Countries acted in a coordinated manner. Moving together, they delivered a global fiscal stimulus of 2 percent of GDP in 2009, exactly what we asked for a year ago. Although the coordination was not explicit, policymakers all did the same thing at the same time for the same reason. This was unprecedented, even if countries did not always receive due credit for this achievement. We are already seeing the payoff — IMF analysis suggests that the fiscal expansion boosted growth by between 1 and 3 percentage points this year, and up to a third of the gain comes explicitly from coordination.

However as the crisis unfolded and its persistent and pervasive nature became clear, it was recognised that the coverage of the coordination process had to be considerably widened to include the G20 group and the scope extended to include not only monetary and fiscal policy but also financial sector regulation and supervision. The main partners in such a coordinated approach would be

1. National regulatory and supervisory authorities;
2. IMF;
3. Financial Stability Board (FSB) and other international standard setting bodies (Basel Committee on Banking Supervision or BCBS, International Organisation of Securities Commissions or IOSCO) etc.;
4. Influential groups like G20.

Role of National Regulatory and Supervisory Authorities

The role of national regulatory and supervisory authorities was debated extensively first in the de Larosière Group (Feb 2009) in the EU and then in the Working Group 1 of the G20 (March 2009). The deliberations threw considerable light on the existing deficiencies in the global financial system and suggested several measures to mitigate the possibility of recurrences of a crisis of such an amplitude. The suggested measures embraced five distinct areas, viz.

1. Expanding the scope of regulation;
2. Issues related to the leverage of financial institutions;
3. Pro-cyclicality of capital requirements;
4. Reducing costs of financial failures;
5. Devising market incentives for prudential behaviour.

Scope of regulation

It was felt that regulation not only has to be strengthened but its scope extended considerably. For strengthening regulation two measures seem to be in order, viz. (i) entrusting a special regulatory authority (either an existing one or a newly constituted one) with an explicit financial stability mandate and (ii) ensuring coordination between different regulatory authorities. The scope of regulation needs to be extended to include credit rating agencies and private pools of capital (including hedge funds) via a system of registration, disclosure requirements and oversight.

Leverage of financial institutions

An important amplification factor for the current crisis has been not only the high degree of leveraging of many financial institutions but also the fact that this leveraging has very often been quite opaque. Simpler leverage measures are necessary to supplement the Basel Tier 1 and 2 requirements (such as a minimum unweighted leverage ratio for bank capital). Considering the phenomenal growths of off-balance-sheet activities (e.g. contingency banking and financial engineering products, securitisation of bank assets, loan sales, etc.), there is need for more accurate measures of balance sheet exposures. As part of the latter, one should expect a stronger focus by regulators on loan-to-value ratios (especially for mortgages) and higher loan-loss provisioning norms. Stress testing exercises should be conducted periodically to monitor leveraging on an ongoing basis, accompanied by improved disclosure requirements for complex structured products.

Pro-cyclicality of capital requirements

A fact well-known to economists (see e.g. Ghosh and Nachane, 2003) but consistently ignored by policymakers is the fact of capital adequacy requirements being pro-cyclical and hence a possible accentuating factor in any crisis. As the current crisis runs its course, there is a greater realisation among central bankers globally that ways have to be found for countering this pro-cyclicality. The first step in such an endeavour would be to encourage the build-up of capital buffers during economic expansions. These could then be unwound in times of recession to forestall the adverse impacts of fair valuation, leverage and maturity mismatches. There is also the necessity of imposing higher capital requirements on systemically important financial institutions.

Reducing cost of financial failures

The welfare costs of financial crises are generally severe and fall disproportionately on disadvantaged groups in any society, and the current crisis is hardly an exception. An early warning diagnostic system can contribute considerably towards containing collateral damage. In this regard the Prompt Corrective Action (PCA) scheme introduced by the RBI in December 2002 is noteworthy.[10] Another

---

[10] Under the PCA, the RBI will initiate certain *structured* as well as *discretionary* actions in respect of banks, which have hit certain trigger points in terms of capital adequacy ratio (CAR), net non-performing assets (NPA) and return on assets (ROA). Thus if a bank's CAR falls to less than 9 percent, but equal or more than 6 percent, then the RBI will initiate the following structured actions: (i) Submission and implementation of capital restoration plan by the bank; (ii) Bank will restrict expansion of its risk-weighted assets; (iii) Bank will not enter into new lines of business; (iv) Bank will not access/renew costly deposits and CDs; (v) Bank will reduce/skip dividend payments. In addition it could also initiate any of the following discretionary actions: (i) RBI will order recapitalisation; (ii) Bank will not increase its stake in subsidiaries; (iii) Bank will reduce its exposure to sensitive sectors like capital market, real estate or investment in non-SLR securities.

important measure relates to the prevalence of orderly closure rules for important financial institutions (as prevalent in the US for banks under the FDIC Improvement Act and Competitive Equality Banking Act). Under exceptionally turbulent circumstances, the use of credit ratings by private agencies could be temporarily suspended in favour of regulators' ratings. A final and critical step could be to establish clearing houses in OTC derivatives markets and make such central counterparties subject to transparent and effective oversight.

Devising market incentives for prudent behaviour

Market incentives can play an important supplementary role in ensuring prudent behaviour by financial institutions. It is generally recognised that an important triggering factor in the current crisis was the unregulated corporate compensation framework, which provided perverse incentives for excessive risk taking, resulting in a serious moral hazard syndrome. The solution to this proposed by Working Group 1 of the G20 is prudential oversight of financial executive compensation schemes. If this is found difficult to implement, a softer option seems to be to put in place a deferred compensation plan to replace the existing practice of paying bonuses up-front to top management. To reduce the opaqueness associated with securitisation, originators of securitised products may be required to take an equity slice in the products that they sell/distribute. Credit rating agencies face important conflicts of interest between their ratings and consultancy activities and hence there is a need for better separation of these two functions. A very interesting suggestion for market-induced discipline in financial institutions is the so-called Chicago Fed Plan (see Keehn, 1989), which argues for the inclusion of a mandatory subordinated debt component in bank capital (detailed discussion of this Plan and several variants may be found in Calomiris and Powell, 2000; Evanoff and Wall, 2000; etc.).[11]

---

[11] In India there is no mandatory requirement for subordinate debt, but there is a ceiling (<50 percent of Tier 1 capital). Such debt is part of Tier 2 capital.

Revised Role of the IMF

In the aftermath of every crisis there is always in evidence a general dissatisfaction with the IMF's role as the sole global resolution mechanism. This dissatisfaction is particularly acute among LDCs and EMEs, but is not confined to them alone. Even the advanced group of countries would like to see some reforms getting under way and of course there are several reform areas which exercise both groups in equal measure. By and large the various suggestions for IMF reforms may be grouped under the following headings:

1. *Replacement of ex-post (crisis) negotiations on IMF loan conditions with ex-ante rules for IMF membership.* This would imply that only those countries which agree to certain conditions *ab initio* would qualify for IMF assistance in the event of a crisis. The rationale for this measure is that it would induce countries to adopt preventive measures well in advance of crisis situations, thus mitigating their severity or even forestalling their occurrence. Such a solution if implemented secretly would severely isolate economies which for some reason refuse to be signatories to this arrangement, and would in effect be tantamount to ostracizing certain economies from the global financial community. The *ex-ante* conditions suggested include:

   (i)   Subordinated debt requirements;
   (ii) Minimum reserve ratios for banks and other financial institutions;
   (iii) (Risk-based) deposit insurance (for banks and other financial institutions);
   (iv) Free entry to foreign banks;
   (v)   No regulatory bias in favour of off-balance-sheet activities;
   (vi) Regulation and supervision of national regulator to cover all systemically important financial institutions;
   (vii) No scope for regulatory arbitrage, which arises when some components of the financial system are regulated with a "lighter touch" relative to others (as happens for example with NBFCs in India).

2. *A vigorous enforcement of IMF guidelines on exchange rate surveillance.* This will be with special reference to emerging global imbalances, protracted currency undervaluation, currency mismatches, etc.

3. *Lender of "last resort" function of the IMF.* This is essentially a revival of Walter Bagehot's 19th century proposal of what a lender of last resort should ideally do in the event of a banking crisis. It is proposed that the IMF should lend freely during crises on good collateral at a penalty rate and for short periods (say less than 90 days) with limited rollover possibilities. Of the collateral, 25 percent could be in the form of foreign government securities and the penal rate could be 2 percent above the value-weighted yield on the bundle of securities offered as collateral (see Calomiris, 2007; Goldstein, 2008; Brunnermeier and Pedersen, 2009; etc.).

4. *More adequate representation of the LDCs' and EMEs' points of view.* There has been long-standing and simmering discontent among the LDCs and EMEs that the IMF does not provide adequate representation of their point of view. Their main demands are threefold:

   (i)   Radical changes in access, pricing and conditionality for IMF borrowers, in particular the introduction of flexible credit lines;
   (ii) Raising quotas/votes of EMEs and LDCs as a group;[12]
   (iii) Negating the US veto on crucial IMF decisions.

It is to be noted that the Committee on IMF Governance Reform (under the Chairmanship of Trevor Manuel), which submitted its Report in March 2009, has made an honest effort to address several

---

[12] A proposed tripling of basic votes (number of votes every country has *qua* member) would increase developing country votes from 32.3 to 34.4 percent (the corresponding World Bank figure is 42.6 percent, proposed to be raised to 43.8 percent). Birdsall (2009) makes a particularly relevant suggestion in this context, viz. double majority voting on selected issues — a majority of weighted votes (as currently) + a majority of countries. The system prevails at the Inter-American Development Bank, ADB, African Development Bank for election of a new president/head.

of these concerns, though whether the suggestions will be finally incorporated in the IMF Charter is as yet unclear. Among the major recommendations of the Report are the following:

1. An accelerated quota revision process to be concluded by April 2010;
2. Expansion of the Fund surveillance mandate beyond exchange rates to macro-prudential issues, financial spillovers and capital account policies;
3. Lowering of the voting threshold on critical decisions from 85 percent to 70–75 percent. This would in effect annul the US veto (as the US has 17 percent voting power);
4. Extending double majority to a wider range of decisions;
5. Greater transparency and role for merit in the appointment of the Managing Director and Deputy Managing Directors.

Role of the Financial Stability Board (FSB) and Other International Standard Setting Bodies

The Financial Stability Forum (FSF) was established in 1999, by the Finance Ministers and Central Bank Governors of the G7 to promote international financial stability through enhanced information exchange and international co-operation in financial market surveillance. The FSF, being heavily dominated by G7 representation, excluded the concerns of much of the rest of the world including key emerging Asian economies such as China, India, Indonesia, Korea, Malaysia and Thailand. In April 2009, the FSF gave way to the Financial Stability Board (FSB) with an extended membership of countries (G20 + Spain + European Commission) and an expanded mandate. Several roles are envisaged for the FSB, of which the following four seem to be of particular importance:

1. Alert standard setting bodies about loopholes in existing regulatory structures. Bodies like BCBS and IOSCO can then devise specific operational guidelines for incorporation into national regulatory and surveillance frameworks.

2. Monitor and advise on market developments and their implications for regulatory policy.
3. Develop an early warning system on emerging systemic risks when the situation so warrants (Brunnermeier *et al.*, 2009). This could be done in collaboration with the IMF.
4. Manage contingency plans for cross-border crisis management particularly with respect to systemically important multinational firms.

Role of the G20

In recent years the G20 has emerged as an influential group for directing the thrust of globally coordinated policy, though it must be mentioned that it is purely a consultative and advisory forum with no operational status. In spite of this last limitation, the G20 did contribute substantially to toning down some of the more serious consequences of the current crisis. Among its major achievements since the inception of the current crisis have been (i) succeeding in securing a substantial increase in IMF resources ($750 bn + $250 bn SDR allocation) and also of the MDBs' ($100 bn); (ii) ensuring a greater degree of flexibility in IMF support programmes (flexible credit lines); (iii) strengthening financial supervision and regulation (regulatory oversight of credit rating agencies, action against non-co-operative jurisdictions and tax havens, improving accounting standards, establishment of a new Financial Stability Board (FSB) etc.); (iv) supporting growth in EMEs and LDCs by helping to finance countercyclical spending, bank recapitalisation, infrastructure, etc; (v) countering rising protectionism; and finally (vi) reaffirming the Millennium Development Goals.

An interesting proposal which may at some stage be usefully espoused by the G20 pertains to the group insurance scheme (for G20 members) proposed by E. Prasad (2009). The broad contours of the scheme are as follows: (i) participants to be offered a short-term credit line in the event of a crisis; (ii) entry fee between $10 bn to $20 bn; (iii) premium to depend on the level of insurance desired and a suggested value is 1 percent of the face value of the policy;

(iv) countries following policies that enhance global risk (such as large budget or current account deficits) would face higher premia; (v) premia to be invested in US, euro area and Japanese government bonds, and in return the central banks of these countries would top up the lines of credit in the event of a global crisis; (vi) the scheme to be administered by the FSB rather than the IMF since the voting in the former is not based on country quota subscriptions (as is the case with the latter).[13]

Official Thinking on Future Course of Financial Sector Reforms in India: A Critique

Indian policymakers in the highest circles have been reaffirming their commitments to financial sector reforms, particularly so after the UPA government's return to power in July 2009. But these statements are too vague to offer any direct clue about the actual course of reforms over the next few years. But one has reason to suppose that the future roadmap of reforms will closely follow the recommendations outlined in the reports of two recent committees — the Committee on Making Mumbai an International Finance Centre (IFC) under the chairmanship of Percy Mistry and the Committee on Financial Sector Reforms (CFSR for short) under the chairmanship of Raghuram Rajan. The latter report in particular is a detailed examination of the Indian financial sector, and makes a number of wide-ranging recommendations.

Let me begin by mentioning that there are several issues taken up by the CFSR with which I am in broad agreement, such as those related to broadening access to finance (Proposals 3 and 4), a level playing field (Proposal 8), developing credit infrastructure (Proposals 29 and 30) and improvement of land registration and titling (Proposals 31 and 32).

---

[13] The G20 Insurance Solution has several points of similarity with the Chiang Mai Initiative of the ASEAN+3.

However, I have serious reservations about some of the substantive issues that have been raised in the CFSR. I will group my comments under four major headings:

1. The general philosophy about financial markets espoused by the Report;
2. The macroeconomic framework;
3. Principles versus rules-based regulation; and
4. Regulatory and supervisory independence (RSI).

On the first of these, it needs to be emphasized that the entire CFSR approach is strongly grounded in the *new classical* (or *freshwater*) view of financial markets, about which several reservations have been noted in a previous section, particularly in the wake of the current crisis.[14] Hence these need not be repeated here. Let me however briefly touch upon the remaining issues.

Macroeconomic framework

The two aspects of the macroeconomic framework suggested by the CFSR which have attracted most attention are *inflation targeting* (IT) and *capital account convertibility* (CAC).

The main policy recommendation of the CFSR as regards a suitable monetary policy regime for India pertain to the announcement of a "low inflation objective — a number, a number that can be brought down over time, or a range — over a medium term horizon (say two years) as the primary goal of monetary policy" (Report of the CSFR). In the execution of this objective the RBI would be granted full operational independence and simultaneously held fully accountable. This recommendation is in tune with current mainstream academic thinking, so in a way the CFSR is only reiterating the orthodox position. To many, including the top brass in the US

---

[14] My own reservations about this approach have pre-dated the crisis (see Nachane, 2007).

Fed and the ECB (including such notables as Alan Greenspan, Otmar Issing, Donald Kohn, etc.), IT appears an idea whose time is yet to come, but even those who regard it as a desirable long-term goal admit that the devil lies in the details. Where the CFSR falls short of expectations is in its failure to convince the reader of the superiority of IT to the existing (discretionary) monetary policy regime in India and the lack of attention to the specific difficulties that would need to be overcome for operationalizing such a procedure (in the Indian context).

Inflation-targeting central banks typically assume that financial stability is a by-product of price stability. The recent sub-prime crisis in the US, following a long period of steeply appreciating equity and real estate prices, occurring in a period of sustained price stability, should serve as a telling refutation of this position. But this case is by no means unique. The literature (e.g. Bordo *et al.*, 2000; Borio and Lowe, 2002) furnishes several such instances — Japan (1985–89), Korea (1990–97), the US (1925–29), etc. Even the Indian situation of 2005–07 appears similar. The fact of this possible disconnect between asset prices and general inflation could mean that typically an IT central bank may allow credit to expand and feed an asset price boom for too long. Ultimately when the asset price boom feeds into general inflation (via the wealth effect) the central bank would be forced to apply the brakes abruptly, which could result in a prolonged asset price deflation (to wit Japan's "lost decade" of the 1990s) and a general recession. Thus an IT central bank will always intervene too late to prevent a crisis.

There also seems to be an implicit supposition in the CFSR that adoption of IT guards against balance-of-payments crisis. This need not necessarily be so. IT does not insulate a country against balance-of-payments crises (see Calvo and Vegh, 1999; Mendonza and Uribe, 2001; Kumhof *et al.*, 2007; etc.). Such vulnerability could arise from a weak fiscal revenue base, implicit financial bailout guarantees, contingent government liabilities, etc. In short if fiscal discipline is relatively lax, then achieving macroeconomic stability by strict monetary discipline can be counterproductive. The FRBM Act in India does seem to promise an era of fiscal discipline in the future, but in general fiscal discipline seems to be far more difficult to achieve than monetary discipline.[15]

Finally, the empirical evidence on the success of IT regimes is mixed.[16] Ball and Sheridan (2003) find that "there is no evidence that inflation targeting improves performance", whereas Levin *et al.* (2004), Hyvonen (2004) and Vega and Winkelried (2005) report a lowering of inflation persistence and an anchoring of inflationary expectations for ITers.[17]

Let me now turn to the other major issue regarding the macro-economic framework, viz. capital account convertibility (CAC). Here the CFSR makes a strong pitch for an accelerated move in the direction of CAC.[18] As we have mentioned above, there has been in the aftermath of the current crisis a resurgence of interest in the Keynesian view of financial markets (or the so-called *saltwater* view). A logical corollary of this tilt towards Keynesianism has been a great deal of re-thinking on the issue of capital controls — within the academic community as well as in several official circles. Most significant in this context is the revised stance of the IMF on its pet bugbear of capital controls. Capital controls, which had been (particularly since the 1980s) anathema to the IMF's thinking, are now not only admitted, but even actively promoted. As a matter of fact, when Iceland's banking system collapsed in September 2008, a key component of the IMF reform package was "controls on capital outflows". Several countries in Central and Eastern Europe (including Turkey, Russia, Kazakhstan, Ukraine, Poland, Bulgaria, etc.) and

---

[15] The current total fiscal deficit — both central and state and including several contingent liabilities — at 12 percent of GDP may perhaps be regarded as exceptional and likely to be moderated as the fiscal stimulus is wound down.

[16] Countries using some form of IT currently include: Australia, Brazil, Canada, Chile, Colombia, Finland, Mexico, New Zealand, Poland, Sweden, UK, etc.

[17] For a fuller discussion of this viewpoint, kindly refer to Nachane (2008).

[18] Rajan's strong advocacy of CAC contrasts strangely with the pragmatic (and far more nuanced) approach to capital account liberalisation that he espouses (alongwith E.S. Prasad) in the *Journal of Economic Perspectives* (Summer 2008).

Africa have either introduced some form of capital controls or are on the verge of doing so.[19]

Indian policymakers, right from the inception of reforms, have shown tremendous enthusiasm for accelerated capital account liberalisation. The two committees appointed to examine the issue (Tarapore I and II) have laid out a detailed roadmap for full capital account convertibility (CAC). It is important to stress that the line taken by several apologists for CAC, that the risks of financial instability are negligible and hence more than compensated for by the benefits, ignores the magnitude of the potential costs of a crisis which have been carefully noted by Rakesh Mohan (2007). The total welfare costs would be substantially higher given the fact that the poor and vulnerable sections of the society have to bear a disproportionately large share of the costs.

Surprisingly, the pronounced swing of opinion against unfettered capital account liberalisation which has occurred among a majority of academic economists as well as several foreign governments and multilateral institutions (the IMF not excepted) in the light of the recent financial upheavals seems to have completely bypassed Indian policy circles. Indian policymakers need to remember that empirical studies fail to demonstrate any clear and convincing evidence of a favourable impact of capital account convertibility on total factor productivity, economic growth, and poverty reduction — even where such effects are in fact detected, they are circumscribed by a host of conditioning factors including levels of economic development, institutional quality, sequencing of reforms, etc. (see, in particular, the summary evaluation in the recent Report of the BIS Committee on

---

[19] Academic thinking in the highest circles is also veering strongly towards the need for capital controls. To cite but two opinions from a long list: First, Paul Krugman (*The New York Times*, 12 September 2009) has this to say on capital controls: Back in 1998, in the midst of the Asian financial crisis, I came out in favor of temporary capital controls... At the time it was regarded as a horribly unorthodox and irresponsible suggestion... Today, that wild and crazy idea is so orthodox it's part of standard IMF policy". Second, in a recent lecture De Long talks about "the intellectual bankruptcy of the Chicago School" (6th Singapore Economic Review Public Lecture, 7 January. 2009).

the Global Financial System 2009 under the chairmanship of Rakesh Mohan). On the other hand, CAC poses very real threats to financial stability and monetary policy autonomy, especially for countries with weak regulatory mechanisms and undeveloped financial markets (see, in particular, Y.V. Reddy's recent book *India and the Global Financial Crisis* [2009]).

There are several further issues specifically germane to the Indian situation. First, a substantial opening of the capital account has already taken place over the last decade and since (even as its advocates cannot be unaware of), CAC can only convey short-term growth effects (see Henry, 2007), whatever benefits of opening the capital account that were due must have already accrued. Any further opening up of the capital account can only convey marginal benefits while increasing the risks of financial instability substantially. Participatory notes (PNs) also present several problems, most notably related to anti-money laundering and terrorist funding — see the speech by M.K. Narayanan, National Security Advisor, Government of India, at the 43rd Munich Conference on Security Policy (2007). While they do lend considerable liquidity to the stock market, PNs can hardly be viewed as a source of getting long-term funds into India.

Irrespective of whether India decides to go for full CAC or otherwise, management of capital inflows will remain an important issue for some time into the future. One rational policy response would then be to examine a minimal set of capital account restrictions that will mitigate the probability of financial crises of the order of the Asian crisis (1997–1998), the LTCM crisis (1998) or the Russian crisis (1998). Various proposals for managing capital inflows have been made including Tobin taxes, variable deposit requirements, interest equalization taxes, group insurance, etc. Of these the trip wire-speed bump approach (TW-SB) is the one which I find particularly appealing. The essence of this approach is simple. Certain basic indicators (trip wires or TWs) are defined and as and when these indicators deteriorate (below a threshold), certain safety measures (relating to capital account transactions) — speed bumps or SBs — are "triggered off" (see Nachane, 2007). The TW-SB approach has several points of commonality with the early warning system advocated at the recently concluded Pittsburgh Summit of the G20.

Principles versus rules-based regulation

The principles vs rules mode of regulation was first brought into the picture (in the Indian context) by the Committee on Making Mumbai an IFC. The Committee chastized the RBI for the plethora of rules that financial institutions were required to follow and strongly advocated a switchover to a *principles-based* system. The CFSR reiterates the same position but with less rhetoric and greater attention to detail. Principles-based regulation involves greater reliance on "principles and outcome-focused, high-level rules as a means to drive at the regulatory aims we want to achieve, and less reliance on prescriptive rules" (FSA, 2007). Essentially, two concepts are involved, viz. principles restraining regulatory discretion and general guidelines that might supplant the existing detailed rules for auditors and regulated entities. It is the CFSR's contention that the current rules-based system in India displays "low tolerance for innovation and excessive micro-management" (Report of the CFSR, Chapter 6, p. 2). It therefore recommends a gradual but time-bound movement in the direction of principles-based regulation.

There are several imminent problems with the adoption of a principles-based approach for India. At least a few of these deserve to be mentioned.

1. In a principles-based system, the interpretation of principles often lies with the regulator, in contrast to a rules-based system where interpretation lies equally with the regulator and the regulated, with well-defined mechanisms for resolving conflicts of interpretation. Thus, ironically, a principles-based system places greater discretion at the disposal of the regulator. This can often lead to arbitrary regulation, but the greater danger is of attempts by powerful corporate interests at regulatory capture and blocking of competition (the recent Wal-Mart case in the US is an example — see Wallison, 2007).

2. It is not exactly clear whether the CFSR is suggesting a principles-based system only for financial institutions or for the entire corporate sector. Either interpretation is fraught with difficulties. If principles-based regulation is to apply to the entire corporate sector, the details spelt out in the CFSR for implementing such a gigantic scheme are extremely sketchy, being confined to generalities rather than going into specificities. Too much stress on self-regulation and expecting firms to appreciate their own regulatory responsibilities is an unwarranted utopian view of the Indian corporate mentality. If, on the other hand, the CFSR is making the more modest suggestion of a principles-based system for the financial sector, with the existing system largely intact for the non-financial sector, the procedure is more feasible, but will create problems arising from the interface of two distinct systems. In a litigious country like India, the arbitration/judicial system will be overwhelmed with public interest litigations RTI queries and private class actions.

3. Finally, as noted by Wallison (2007), there is the *safe haven* effect of a rules-based system. Compliance with rules which are fully transparent give the regulated entities a sense of absolution, which is never present in a principles-based system. There is, besides, no question of discrimination between different regulated entities in a rules-based system, a problem which is never totally absent in a principles-based system.

All this is hardly to say that the existing rules-based system in India is without defects, and several of these are highlighted effectively in the Report. But instead of a switchover to a principles-based system, a far better alternative is to impart flexibility and dynamism to the existing rules, making them more transparent and installing a system of quick incentives/penalties for compliance/non-compliance.

Regulatory and supervisory independence

The issue of regulatory and supervisory independence (RSI) is often confused with central bank independence (CBI), though as stressed in the literature (see Lastra, 1996; Taylor and Fleming, 1999; Quintyn and Taylor, 2002), the two are conceptually distinct and need not necessarily co-exist even when the regulation and supervision functions and the monetary policy functions are vested in the same authority. In a sense, RSI is to financial stability what CBI is to monetary stability. Unfortunately the academic literature on regulation has been almost exclusively focused on CBI, to the virtual neglect of RSI. The CFSR also fails to touch on this aspect at all, though of course it does pay a great deal of attention to the issue of single versus multiple regulators.[20]

The neglect of RSI assumes importance when one considers the fact that almost all episodes of financial distress have been associated with weak RSI.[21] RSI refers to independence of the regulatory and supervisory structure from not only the government but also from the industry and financial markets. In India the financial regulatory and supervisory functions are distributed between the RBI (banks and NBFCs), state governments (for co-operative financial institutions jointly with RBI) and the National Bank for Agriculture and Rural Development (for RRBs). For the purposes of this discussion let us confine ourselves to the regulation and supervision of the banking sector and the NBFCs. The RBI discharges this function under the guidance of the Board for Financial Supervision (BFS), which comprises four directors from the RBI's Central Board, the RBI Governor (as Chairman) and four Deputy Governors.

As far as independence from the government on the regulatory and supervisory fronts is concerned, this is ensured to a large extent by the fact that the RBI (acting under the guidance of the BFS) is authorised to issue directives in all areas of regulation and supervision. However this realisation has to be tempered by the fact that an element of indirect control by the government does exist by virtue of the

---

[20] The CFSR's preferred regulatory architecture (Proposals 23–28) is one where all depository institutions come under the supervisory purview of the RBI, with a separate agency for supervising large systemically important financial conglomerates.
[21] See De Krivoy (2000) for the Venezuelan experience of the mid-1990s, Lindgren *et al.* (1999) for the East Asian experience, Hartcher (1998) for Japan, etc.

fact that the RBI directors (from whom four of the BFS members are drawn) are appointed by the central government. Incidentally, the CFSR's recommendation to set up the Financial Development Council under the chairmanship of the Finance Minister "for macro-economic assessment and development issues" (Proposal 26), if implemented, will strongly limit the existing independence of the regulators and supervisors, as it will provide a legitimate platform for the Finance Ministry to intervene in these matters, and further exacerbate the coordination problems between the RBI and the Finance Ministry.

But the other major dimension of RSI, viz. independence from markets, is equally important but has not received the attention it deserves. In the words of a very famous US central banker: "it is just as important for a central bank to be independent of markets as it is to be independent of politics" (see Blinder, 1997). Independence from markets is more difficult to ensure than independence from politicians, since the forces operative here are extremely subtle. This can occur primarily through two channels, both of which have been operative in the Indian context. First, an overwhelming preponderance of financial sector and industry representatives in official committees and bodies, concerned with the designing of the regulatory architecture. This usually takes place in the instance of a government strongly committed to reforms, and is usually done with the ostensible purpose of taking on board the "financial industry point of view". Second, large sections of the media are strongly aligned with corporate sector interests and hence by extremely ingenious propaganda manage to create a general impression that national interests are closely conflated with financial sector interests. A grading system is then set up, whereby supervisors and regulators are rated publicly on how friendly they are to markets. We are treading on thin ground here. On the one hand, financial stability is a public good, and financial market development contributes to real development. Yet it is undeniable that exuberance, animal spirits and general short-termism strongly pervade financial markets. A regulatory authority overtly sensitive to financial market demands could be a classic case of what Stigler (1971) has termed *regulatory capture*. Unfortunately the CFSR observes a deafening silence on this vital issue.

A Suggested Agenda

At the outset, let me emphasize that there is a fundamental difference between the crises in the US, EU and India. In the US the crisis originated endogenously within the financial system and then spread from Wall Street to Main Street (to use President Obama's famous expression). In the EU and other Western countries, the financial system was first affected largely by contamination from the US financial system and then the crisis spread to the real economy. In India (and some other Asian countries) the primary source of contagion has been via the trade channel, so the real sector has been affected to a great extent but the financial system remains intact. It is true that sporadic evidence of exposure of domestic private sector banks (in India) as well as some nationalised banks and foreign subsidiaries to the so-called toxic assets and CDOs in the US and EU has come to light from time to time, but the extent of total exposure is likely to be limited to something like US$1.5 bn (on a mark-to-market basis). A substantial share of the credit for the robustness of the Indian financial system must go to the former RBI Governor Y.V. Reddy for carefully monitoring the securitisation processs in India and forestalling the emergence of asset bubbles feeding on indiscriminate credit expansion. The *New York Times* (20 December 2008) came closest to the mark when it described him as "the right man in the right job at the right time". Given that the recessions in the US, EU and India represent three distinct patterns, the nature of the Indian policy response should not necessarily track theirs, but should be specially designed to account for the specificities of our situation. In particular, three concerns should be paramount in the Indian context, viz.

1. *Revival sans stagflation.* First, there is, of course, the need to revive the real economy without, in the process, unleashing forces that could trigger a future asset and/or commodity price inflation.
2. *Firewalls around the financial sector.* As mentioned above, since the Indian crisis is largely an imported one (primarily via the trade and investment routes) and, further, since the financial sector

has been more or less secure so far, policy should emphasise the insulation of the Indian financial sector from adverse shocks originating either in the Indian real sector or in the financial systems of the US and EU.

3. *Safety nets for the vulnerable sections.* As the ILO's *Global Employment Report* (Jan 2009) points out, in a classic moral twist to the global crisis tale, those who had the least to do with the perpetration of the crisis (namely, the vulnerable sections of society across the globe) are being forced to bear the brunt of the consequences. India is no exception, and hence a necessary third pillar of any anti-recessionary strategy should be to build extensive safety nets for those at maximum risk of exposure to collateral damage.

Indian policy in the aftermath of the crisis[22] has been addressed almost exclusively to the first objective, with attention to the second confined mainly towards bank capitalisation (see footnote 15), while the last objective has largely languished in the domain of rhetoric.

---

[22] The policy measures so far adopted in India may be summed up in a single phrase — easy money and fiscal stimuli. On the monetary policy front there has been a flurry of activity — the repo rate was reduced in a succession of steps from the level of 9 percent in September 08 to 5 percent in March 09 (with a corresponding reduction in the reverse repo rate from 6 to 3.5 percent), the CRR was also reduced from 9 to 5 percent over the same period, whereas the SLR was brought down by 1 to 24 percent. Altogether, it has been estimated that these measures have released more than Rs. 400,000 crores (US$80 bn approximately) of liquidity into the system. There have also been three successive fiscal stimuli packages amounting to a total cost of Rs. 80,100 crores (US$16.3 bn) to the Exchequer. Fiscal Stimulus I (7 Dec 08) mainly comprised an across-the-board cut of 4 percent in excise duty (estimated cost: Rs. 31,000 crores). Fiscal Stimulus II (2 Jan 09) comprised Rs. 20,000 crores towards bank capitalisation over the next two years, as well as providing greater market borrowing access to state governments and the IIFCL (India Infrastructure Financing Co. Ltd.) (estimated cost: Rs. 70,000 crores). The final Stimulus III (24 Feb 09) provides a 2 percent reduction in both the excise duty and the service tax and an extension of the previous excise duty cuts beyond 31 March 09 (estimated cost: Rs. 29,100 crores). The total burden on the Exchequer at Rs. 81,000 crores amounts to nearly 1.82 percent of the 2008–09 GDP (at current prices) or 2.57 percent (at constant prices).

A policy package, in consonance with the three objectives set out above, would be one that includes the following specific measures.

1. Any further monetary policy easing or fiscal stimulus runs the grave danger of laying the foundation for a future high inflation phase. Given the long lags in monetary and fiscal policy[23] (between two to three quarters), the effects of the policy measures taken so far are likely to take effect towards end 2009, just about the time when the excess capacity in the economy is estimated to be working itself out.

2. There is no denying that the failure of credit delivery to micro, small and medium enterprises (MSMEs) is having systemically important effects in delaying the recovery and in aggravating social distress due to job losses, etc. It is now time to strike out boldly by attempting measures like government guarantees of loans to MSMEs on the lines of the Mandelson Plan in the UK (Lord Mandelson, Business Secretary, UK Government, has announced plans to guarantee bank loans to SMEs with sales of up to £500 mn). Actually there is provision for credit guarantees under the Deposit Insurance and Credit Guarantee Corporation (DICGC) Act 1961. However this has now become defunct (see DICGC Annual Report 2007–08, p. 1). The DICGC needs to be strengthened with an infusion of funds and entrusted with the responsibility of administering such a scheme.

3. There already exist provisions for special treatment of risk weights on loans to MSMEs under Basel II. The provisions envisage exemption of loans to MSMEs from capital requirements (or at least assigning these loans a lower risk relative to larger-size firms in the same ratings category).

4. As a purely temporary measure, for the duration of the crisis, loans above a certain limit to industries in sensitive sectors can be tied to some employment protection guarantees.

---

[23] No systematic estimates of these lags are available in the Indian case. Some work in progress currently by the author estimates the lags in monetary policy at around 8 months and for fiscal policy at around 12 months. However these estimates have yet to be firmed up.

5. Encouraging innovative schemes like SME Care and SME Help (initiated by the SBI) for adoption by other banks on an extensive scale.[24]

6. Financial crises affect vulnerable sections of society (including labour) far more than non-vulnerable sections. Hence, in the interest of such sections, ensuring against financial contagion should receive top priority. The general monetary and fiscal measures undertaken so far contribute very little to this objective, with the possible exception of the bank capitalisation provisions under Fiscal Stimulus II. But bank capitalisation is not an insurance against a crisis — it is at best a damage-limitation measure in the event of a crisis actually occurring. Hence there is need for several prudential and "fire fighting" measures such as:

   (a) A switchover to a system of risk-based deposit insurance relying on a system of fair value accounting.[25]

   (b) A raising of the deposit insurance coverage from the current Rs. 1 lakh to Rs. 5 lakhs. This will provide a much-needed safety net for the savings of the middle classes.[26]

   (c) The role of rating agencies in the perpetration of the current crisis has come under heavy scrutiny from economists like Buiter (2008), Portes (2008), Giovanni and Spaventa (2008), etc. Such criticism has prompted the Financial Stability Forum (now the Financial Stability Board), through the IOSCO, to offer a code of conduct for credit rating agencies. The RBI should see that this code of conduct is accepted and adhered to by major credit rating agencies in their Indian operations.

---

[24] Under SME Care, MSME borrowers (with fund-based limits of up to Rs. 10 cr.) can avail additional working capital of up to 20 percent of their existing fund-based limits, wheras under SME Help a five-year tenured loan is extendable for MSMEs with a liberal margin of 15 percent for financing capital expenditure. Both schemes offer loans at a concessional rate of 8 percent during the first year. These concessional schemes are mainly in the areas of pharmaceuticals, food processing and light engineering goods.

[25] Such fair value accounting could be along the lines of SFAS No. 133 issued by the US Financial Accounting Standards Board in 1998.

[26] The concept of middle class used here corresponds to that employed in Sengupta, Kannan and Raveendran (2008).

(d) A strict monitoring of off-balance-sheet items and structured product vehicles (SPVs) of banks and financial institutions.

(e) There is need to recognize that substantive capital flows (in either direction) have potentially strong destabilising consequences. In such circumstances it is necessary to reserve for ourselves the right to impose key capital controls on a pre-announced basis for specified periods of time. The extent and duration of these controls could be related to the setting off of certain macroeconomic triggers. This TW-SB approach is elaborated at length in my earlier paper (Nachane, 2007).[27] The fact that Brazil introduced a Tobin tax of 2 percent on capital inflows shows that at least some EMEs are convinced of the merits of this approach.

(f) One of the most effective safety nets for the poor has been suggested by the National Commission for Enterprises in the Unorganised Sector (NCEUS). This involves the setting up of a National Fund for the Unorganised Sector (NAFUS). The Fund is proposed to have an authorised capital of Rs. 1000 cr. and would be designed to provide (i) refinance to banks and other financial institutions to supplement their efforts to provide credit to unorganised sector enterprises with investment in plant and machinery below Rs. 25 lakhs, but with a special focus on enterprises with investment less than Rs. 5 lakhs; (ii) microfinance support through NGOs, SHGs, MFIs, etc.;

---

[27] In direct contrast to this view, we have a substantially influential group of Indian economists who see in the crisis an opportunity for introducing capital account convertibility. Thus Lahiri in his P.T. Memorial Lecture (16 Jan 09) said,

The current crisis may provide an opportunity for introducing capital account convertibility.

The dominant worry about introducing convertibility has been an upsurge of capital flows with large upward pressure on the exchange rate of the rupee followed by a sudden sucking out of such a capital, precipitating a crisis. Risk aversion on the part of international investors is an all-time high now, and the risk of large inflows is limited.

Not all of us may be persuaded by this somewhat convoluted logic, though it seems to have provided considerable grist to the mill for several professional bloggers!

and (iii) venture capital for innovative enterprises in the unorganised sector. This suggestion of the NCEUS requires an extremely serious consideration from the government, though there are no signs that this is happening.

Conclusion

While there is no denying the fact that financial system development is an integral component of overall development, there are important caveats to this general statement. The current financial crisis has exposed some clear fault lines in unchecked financial innovation and deregulation. In particular, opinion seems to be swinging away from the pristine view of free markets evident in classical laissez faire, to the more nuanced view of Keynes. This shift in thinking has challenged several established orthodoxies, and as economists grapple to resolve their controversies, policymakers are struggling to find solutions to hitherto unencountered problems. Robert Posner's recent article (2009) is an honest admission of the profession's confusion, wherein he says,

> We have learned since September that the present generation of economists has not figured out how the economy works. The vast majority of them were blindsided by the housing bubble and the ensuing banking crisis; and misjudged the gravity of the economic downturn that resulted... By now a majority of economists are in general agreement with the Obama administration's exceedingly Keynesian strategy for digging the economy out of its deep hole.

But as the global economy is slowly emerging from the crisis, certain things are becoming clear — in particular the inconsistencies in regulatory systems across countries and the clear conflicts of interests between regulators across borders as well as between regulators and financial markets. A new era of global financial coordination to deal with global systemic risk seems to be dawning. But this will have to contend with four formidable and fundamental issues, viz. (i) the coordination of regulations; (ii) coordination of resolution tools; (iii) coordination in depositor and investor protection; and (iv) enhanced information sharing.

The global coordination process would essentially involve four main partners, viz.

1. National regulatory and supervisory authorities;
2. IMF
3. Financial Stability Board (FSB) and other international standard setting bodies (BCBS, IOSCO) etc.;
4. Influential groups like G20.

The success of the global coordination process would depend upon how sincerely these four main partners execute their respective mandates.

It is interesting to note that in several EMEs, the fact that the consequences of the crisis have been relatively muted seems to have lulled policymakers into a sense of security and convinced them that the financial liberalisation process can continue in the same vein as before. The Indian case is particularly noteworthy where the revolutionary change in thinking now taking place globally has completely bypassed official policy thinking, which, from all apparent signs, seems to find it difficult to rid itself of the pre-crisis euphoria about financial liberalisation, as encapsulated in the two Tarapore Committee Reports as well as the more recent Percy Mistry and Raghuram Rajan Reports. India (along with other countries in South Asia) has the unique opportunity to benefit from the lessons learned from the current crisis, most of whose fall-out has been on the developed economies of the West. I cannot resist quoting an old Confucian adage: "Any fool can learn from his own mistakes. It takes a truly wise man to learn from the mistakes of others". Will policymakers in these countries show that kind of wisdom?

References

Alcala, F. and A. Ciccone (2004). "Trade and productivity", *Quarterly Journal of Economics* 119(2): 612–645.

Archer, D. (2006). "Implications of recent changes in banking for the conduct of monetary policy", BIS Papers No. 28 p. 123–151.

Ashcraft, A. and T. Schuerman (2008). *Understanding the Securitization of Subprime Mortgage Credit.* Staff Report No. 318, Federal Reserve Bank of New York (March).

Ball, L.M. and N. Sheridan (2003). "Does inflation targeting matter?", IMF Working Paper No. 03/129.

Birdsall, N. (2009). "IMF governance reform committee report leaves much to the imagination", Centre for Global Development (6 April).

BIS (Committee on the Global Financial System — CGFS) (2009). "Capital flows and emerging market economies", CGFS Paper No. 33.

Blinder, A.S. (1997). "What central bankers could learn from academics — and vice versa", *Journal of Economic Perspectives* 11(2): 3–19.

Bordo, M., M. Dueker and D. Wheelock (2000). "Aggregate price shocks and financial stability: An historical analysis", NBER Working Paper No. 7652.

Borio, C. and P. Lowe (2002). "Asset prices, financial and monetary stability: Exploring the nexus", BIS Working Paper No. 114.

Brunnermeier, M.K. (2009). "Deciphering the liquidity and credit crunch 2007–2008", *Journal of Economic Perspectives* 23(1): 77–100.

Brunnermeier, M., A. Crockett, C. Goodhart, A. Persaud and H. Shin (2009). "Fundamental principles of financial regulation", Geneva Reports on the World Economy, 11 January.

Brunnermeier, M.K. and L.H. Pedersen (2009). "Market liquidity and funding liquidity", *Review of Financial Studies* 22(6): 2201–2238.

Buiter, W. (2009). Regulating the new financial sector", *VoxEu* (9 March) (http://www.voxeu.org/index.php?q=node/3232).

Buiter, W.H. (2008). "Housing wealth isn't wealth" NBER Working Paper No. 14204.

Calomiris, C.W. (2007). "Bank failures in theory and history: The Great Depression and Other 'Contagious' Events", NBER Working Paper No. 13597, National Bureau of Economic Research.

Calomiris, C.W. and A. Powell (2000). "Can emerging market bank regulators establish credit discipline? The case of Argentina 1992–99", NBER Working Paper No. 7715.

Calvo, G. and C. Vegh (1999). "Inflation stabilization and BOP crises in developing countries", in J.B. Taylor and M. Woodford (eds), *Handbook of Macroeconomics*, Vol. 1C, Amsterdam: Elsevier-North Holland.

Claessens, S. (2009). "The financial crisis and financial nationalism", Joint World Bank-CEPR Conference, Brussels (May 26–27).

De Krivoy, R. (2000). *Collapse: The Venezuelan Banking Crisis of '94*, Washington, DC: Group of Thirty.

De Larosière Group (2009). *Report of the High-Level Group on Financial Supervision in the EU*, Brussels (Feb).

De Long, J.B. (2009). "What has happened to Milton Friedman's Chicago School?", 6th Singapore Economic Review Public Lecture (7 January).

Demirguc-Kunt, A. and E. Detragiache (1998). "Financial liberalization and financial fragility", IMF Working Paper No. 98/83.

Eichengreen, B. (2001). "The EMS crisis in retrospect", CEPR Discussion Paper No. 2704.

Evanoff, D. and L. Wall (2000). "Subordinated debt and bank capital reform" FRB Atlanta Working Paper No. 2000–24.

G20 (2009). *Enhancing Sound Regulation and Strengthening Transparency*, Final Report of the G20 Working Group 1.

Ghosh, S. and D. Nachane (2003). "Are Basel capital standards pro-cyclical? Some empirical evidence from India", *Economic and Political Weekly*, 38 (8). 777–784.

Giovanni, A. and L. Spaventa (2008). "Filling the information gap", in A. Felton and C. Reinhart (eds), *The First Global Financial Crisis of the 21st Century*, (http://www.voxeu.org/index.php?q=node/690).

Goldsmith, R. (1969). *Financial Structure and Development*, New Haven, CT: Yale University Press.

Goldstein, M. (2008). "A proposal to improve banks' regulatory liquidity", Financial Times (22 May).

Gorton, G.B. (2008). "The subprime panic", NBER Working Paper No. 14398 (October).

Hartcher, P. (1998) *"The Ministry": How Japan's Most Powerful Institution Endangers World Markets*, Boston, MA: Harvard Business School Press.

Hicks, J. (1969). *A Theory of Economic History*, Clarendon: Oxford Univ. Press.

Hyvonen, M. (2004). "Inflation convergence across countries", Reserve Bank of Australia Research Discussion Paper No. 2004–04.

Kahneman, D. and A. Tversky (1984). "Choices, values and frames", *American Psychologist* 39(4): 341–350.

Kaufmann, D., A. Kraay and H. Mastruzzi (2007). "Governance matters VI : Governance indicators for 1996–2006", World Bank Policy Research Discussion Paper 4280.

Keehn, S. (1989). *Banking on the Balance: Powers and the Safety Net*, Chicago: Federal Reserve Bank of Chicago.

Krugman, P. (2009). "A dark age of macroeconomics (wonkish)", *The New York Times* (27 Jan).

Kumhof, M., S. Li and I. Yan (2007). "Balance of payments crises under inflation targeting", IMF Working Paper No. 84.

Lastra, R.M. (1996). *Central Banking and Banking Regulation*, Financial Markets Group, Lovidon LSE.

LeRoy, S.F. and R.D. Porter (1981). "The present value relation: Tests based on implied variance bounds", *Econometrica* 49(3): 555–574.

Levin, A.T., F. Natalucci and J. Piger (2004). "The macroeconomic effects of inflation targeting", *FRB of St. Louis Review* 86(4): 51–80.

Levine, R. (1997). "Financial development and economic growth: Views and agenda", *Journal of Economic Literature* 15: 688–726.

Lindgren, C., T. Balino, C. Enoch, A. Gulde, M. Quintyn and L. Teo (1999). "Financial sector crisis and restructuring: Lessons from Asia", IMF Occasional Paper No. 188.

Lucas, R. (1988). "On the mechanics of economic development", *Journal of Monetary Economics* 22(1): 3–42.

Meier, G. and D. Seers (eds) (1984). *Pioneers in Development*, New York: Oxford Univ. Press.

Mendonza, E. and M. Uribe (2001). "The business cycles of balance-of-payments crises: A revision of the Mundellian framework", in G. Calvo *et al.* (eds), *Money, Capital Mobility and Trade: Essays in Honour of Robert A. Mundell*, Camb, MA: MIT Press.

Mohan, R. (2007). "Capital account liberalization and conduct of monetary policy: The Indian experience", paper presented at a seminar on Globalization, Inflation and Financial Markets (Banque de France, Paris, France, 14 June).

Nachane, D. (2007). "Liberalisation of the capital account: Perils and possible safeguards", *Economic and Political Weekly* 42(36): 3633–3643.

Nachane, D. (2008). "Committee on financial sector reforms: A critique", *Economic and Political Weekly.* 43(32): 3633–3643.

Nachane, D. and M.S. Islam (2009). "Financial sector reforms in South Asia: A perspective", in T.Y. Tan (ed.), *South Asia: Societies in Political and Economic Transition*, pp. 351–431, Delhi: Manohar Publications.

Narayanan, M.K. (2007). Address at the 43rd Munich Conference on Security Policy (11 February).

Portes, R. (2008). "Ratings agency reforms", in A. Felton and C. Reinhart (eds), *The First Global Financial Crisis of the 21st Century* (http://www.voxeu.org/index.php?q=node/690).

Posner, R. (2009). "How I became a Keynesian", *The New Republic* (23 September).

Prasad, E. (2009). "The risk of a resurgence of global imbalances", *Economic Times* (14 Sept).

Prasad, E.S. and R. Rajan (2008). "A pragmatic approach to capital account liberalization", *Journal of Economic Perspectives* 2(3): 149–172.

Quintyn, M and M.W. Taylor (2002). "Regulatory and supervisory independence and financial stability", IMF Working Paper No. WP/02/46.

Rabin, M. and R.H. Thaler (2001). "Anomalies: Risk aversion", *Journal of Economic Perspectives* 15(1): 219–232.

Reddy, Y.V. (2009). *India and the Global Financial Crisis*, Delhi: Orient Blackswan.

Robinson, J. (1952). *The Rate of Interest and Other Essays*, London: Macmillan.

Rodrik, D., A. Subramanian and F. Trebbi (2002). "Institutions rule: The primacy of institutions over geography and integration in economic development", NBER Working Paper 9305.

Saidane, D. (2002). "The role of financial liberalization in development: Weaknesses and corrections", *Savings and Development* 26(3): 259–276.

Schumpeter, J. (1912). *The Theory of Economic Development.* Trans. O. Redvers, Camb, MA: Harvard Univ. Press (1934).

Seers, D. (1983). *The Political Economy of Nationalism,* New York: Oxford Univ. Press.

Sengupta, A., K.P. Kannan and G. Raveendran (2008). "India's common people: who are they, how many are they and how do they live?", *Economic and political weekly* 43(11): 49–63.

Shiller, R.J. (1981). "Do stock prices move too much to be justified by subsequent changes in dividends?", *American Economic Review* 71(3): 421–436.

Shleifer, A. and L.H. Summers (1990). "The noise trader approach to finance", *Journal of Economic Perspectives* 4(1): 19–33.

Stern, N. (1989). "The economics of development: A survey", *Economic Journal* 99: 597–685.

Stigler, G. (1971). "The theory of economic regulation", *Bell Journal of Economics and Management Science* 6(2): 114–141.

Taylor, M. and A. Fleming (1999). "Integrated financial supervision: Lessons from Northern European experience", World Bank Policy Research Paper No. 2223.

Vega, M. and D. Winkelried (2005). "Inflation targeting and inflation behaviour: A successful story?", *International Journal of Central Banking* 1(3): 153–175.

Wallison, P.J. (2007). "America will prefer to rely on rules, not principles", *Financial Times* (6 July).

Chapter 3

Socio-Economic Developments in South Asia: Issues and Outlook

Mani Shankar Aiyar

South Asia is Prospering; South Asians are Not

This is the central issue of socio-economic development in South Asia.[1] And how it is resolved will determine the outlook for the sub-continent, not only in economic and social terms but, crucially, in terms of domestic political stability, intra-regional relations and the influence of the region and its individual national constituents on the international polity.

I am, therefore, most grateful to Prof. Tan and his colleagues for affording me this opportunity of addressing such a distinguished gathering of scholars and statesmen on what I regard — and what ISAS appears to regard — as the fundamental question facing each of our South Asian countries and our region as a whole: issues of socio-economic development and the future outlook.

The ISAS conference is taking place at the apposite moment when we have before us the IBRD's World Development Indicators 2009, followed by the UN Human Development Report 2009. Together, these provide us with detailed comparative data on how our countries have fared at the economic level of GDP and per capita growth, on

---

[1] I am defining South Asia as the member states of the South Asian Association for Regional Cooperation (SAARC), comprising Afghanistan, Bangladesh, Bhutan, India, the Maldives, Nepal, Pakistan and Sri Lanka. Arguably, Myanmar and even the Autonomous Region of Tibet, although part of the People's Republic of China, could be included in a more academic definition of South Asia.

the one hand, contrasted against how, on the other, we have fared on the Human Development Index.

The basic paradox revealed is that while all our economies have been growing well (ranging from extraordinarily well to relatively well, Nepal excepted), none of us has recorded any particular distinction in translating accelerated growth into inclusive development.

Thus, for example, over this first millennial decade, India has soared from an annual average GDP growth rate of just about 6 percent in the first decade of reform (1992–1993 to 2001–2002) — dipping to a frightful low of 3.8 percent the following year (2002–2003) — to an annual average rate over the next five years (2003–2008) of 8.84 percent, within kissing distance of 9 percent (but with an estimated dip to 6.7 percent in *annus horribilis* 2008–2009).[2] Bangladesh and Pakistan, running neck and neck, have attained 6 percent and above and Sri Lanka, amazingly, has bettered both, notwithstanding the civil war just ended in its North and East provinces. Even Afghanistan crossed 5 percent in 2006–2007. The relative laggard is Nepal, which has been convulsed in political turmoil for most of the past decade from which it is, happily, now emerging. Unfortunately, the World Bank has not published comparative figures for Bhutan and the Maldives.[3]

By and large, South Asia as a region has not only prospered, the secular trajectory of GDP growth has been definitively raised to a higher plane, and the resilience of these economies is being demonstrated by

---

[2] Govt. of India, *Economic Survey*, 2008–2009, Appendix 1.4, p. A7.
[3] IBRD World Development Indicators 2009, Table 1.1, pp. 14–16.

	GDP % growth 2006–2007
India	9.1
Pakistan	6.0
Bangladesh	6.4
Sri Lanka	6.8
Maldives	…
Afghanistan	5.3
Bhutan	…
Nepal	3.2

their having weathered the recent global economic downturn rather more effectively than the developed world or even South Asia's more prosperous neighbours in Southeast Asia.

Yet, the contrast between average annual growth rates in GDP and average annual growth rates in HDI values is striking. While GDP growth rates have soared from 5 to 9 percent, growth rates in HDI values in South Asia[4] have ranged from a low of just over 0.5 percent (Sri Lanka: medium-term) to a high of just over 2 percent (Nepal: short-term). India, which accounts for much of South Asia, has had a modest increase of 1.32 to 1.36 percent in HDI values over the same period. The Pakistan case runs parallel to India, with Bangladesh marginally better. In general, the South Asian economy has risen out of the slough, but the people of South Asia are still stuck in that slough.

Worse, it would appear that as GDP per capita growth rates rise, there is a levelling off, rather than a commensurate rise, in the growth rates of HDI values. Thus, while India's average annual HDI growth rate over the 27-year "long-term" period has been a modest 1.33 percent, the acceleration of the annual average rate of GDP growth by nearly 4 percentage points in the seven-year "short-term" period has raised HDI values by only a miserly 0.03 percent; indeed, the rise in GDP growth rates in the 17-year "medium-term" period actually resulted in a slight decrease of 0.01 percent

---

[4] Long-term (1980–2007), medium-term (1990–2007) and short-term (2000–2007) trends in average annual growth rates in HDI values:

	Long	Medium	Short
Sri Lanka	0.58	0.62	0.57
Maldives			0.78
India	1.33	1.32	1.36
Pakistan	1.30	1.42	
Bangladesh	1.86	1.96	1.39
Nepal	2.16	1.81	1.46
China	1.37	1.40	1.41

(Extracted from Table G, "Human Development Index Trends", UN HDR 2009 pp. 167–170.)

in HDI values compared to the long-term period. Similar levelling-off is seen in the case of China.

Also, tragically, the higher the HDI ranking, the slower is the rate of improvement in HDI values, Nepal, Bangladesh and Pakistan having performed noticeably better in all three periods than the higher-ranking India or the very much higher-ranking Sri Lanka, the Maldives or China. This amounts to a highly disproportionate creaming off of the initial benefits of growth to the better-off; the worse-off a person is, and therefore the more aching his need, the longer he has to wait for a reduction in income inequality and a rise in access to basic human needs.

This may be alright for developed countries with high HDI values. But when it comes to countries in the medium human development category (in which China and all South Asian countries, bar Afghanistan, fall — and, of course, the low human development countries) it is deeply disturbing that instead of accelerated growth in GDP terms impacting comparably on HDI growth, it seems to be true, as a broad proposition, that the faster the GDP per capita growth, the slower the growth in HDI. When this gets added to the Gini coefficient[5] tending to deteriorate as GDP growth rates rise, social inequality suffers a double whammy: income inequality grows even as the gap in access to basic human needs between the better-off and the worse-off, as measured by the UN HDI, also grows.

An important technical addendum to this general line of argument is that Prof. Pranab Bardhan of Berkeley has persuasively argued

---

[5] Gini index (please note that 0 on this index indicates absolute equality and 100 indicates absolute inequality; so the higher the index the worse the income distribution):

Nepal	47.3
Bhutan	46.8
Sri Lanka	41.1
India	36.8
Pakistan	31.2
Bangladesh	31.0
China	41.5

(Extracted from Table M, "Economy and Inequality", UN HDR 2009 pp. 195–198)

in New Delhi's *Business Standard* of 28 August 2009 that India's Gini coefficient for income inequality has been under-calculated as it is based not on income measurements, as in most other countries, but on the consumption data recorded by the official National Sample Survey (NSS). Based on income data collected by the government-funded but independent think-tank, the National Council of Applied Economic Research (NCAER), Prof. Bardhan believes that in India "the Gini coefficient of income inequality comes to 0.535", that is 53.5 on the Gini index and thus considerably worse than China at 41.5.

Given that the political framework in South Asia ranges from the rampantly democratic (India, Sri Lanka) to progressive democratisation (everywhere else, including Afghanistan), in contrast to the experience of more rigidly disciplined polities like China's (or, indeed, Singapore's), the political implications of growing inequalities are likely to manifest themselves sooner than later, destabilising what is arguably the single greatest achievement of South Asia since independence, which is democracy or at least democratisation, and therefore providing growing space for greater freedom of individual thought as well as greater freedom for collective political action. The rise of Naxal (Maoist) terrorism, amounting almost to insurgency, is an early warning of how rising socio-economic inequalities, discrimination and neglect could lead to extremist violence with not inconsiderable support or, at any rate, acquiescence — possibly even helplessness in the face of the breakdown of state security, law and order — on the part of the poorest and most deprived.[6]

Therefore, there is something slightly bogus about slogans of "India Shining" and "South Asia Rising" filling the air, and the mouth-watering prospect on offer of India overtaking the GDP of the United States by 2050 to join China in attaining global economic superpower status within the lifetime of Asian children born in this decade. If a causal relationship could be established between GDP growth and comparable HDI growth, the growth in GDP per capita

---

[6] Prime Minister Manmohan Singh has, accurately in my view, described the rise of Naxalism in large parts of tribal India as the single most important domestic problem facing the nation. It is a portent not to be ignored.

income would suffice as an index of progress. But if the people are not inclusively made part of the growth process, I am not sure that such growth is either economically or politically sustainable or, more importantly, ethically justifiable.[7]

As an Indian, and one who has held high ministerial office, it is only right that I begin by portraying the reality of my own country before drawing comparisons with my South Asian neighbours.

The World Food Programme tells us that half the world's hungry live in India. Which is the more significant reality: Our being the second-fastest growing economy in the world? Or that notwithstanding that extraordinarily high growth rate we remain a low-income, food-deficit country in which as much as 35 percent of the population consumes less than 80 percent of its minimum human energy requirements, where 9 out of 10 pregnant women suffer from malnutrition and anaemia and, in consequence, 47 percent of children under the age of five are moderately to severely undernourished?[8] The Food and Agriculture Organization tells us that in the five years leading to the turn of the century, India added more newly hungry millions than the rest of the world put together.[9]

On education inequality, I can hardly better Prof. Bardhan:

> Most people don't know that India's educational inequality is one
> of the worst in the world: according to World Bank estimates, the

---

[7] Cf. R. Radhakrishna and S. Chandrasekhar, *"Overview — Growth: Achievements and Distress"*, in *India Development Report 2008*, (New Delhi: OUP, 2008) "...there has been no significant acceleration in the process of poverty reduction in 1980–2005 despite an acceleration in the growth of per capita GDP". (Growth and Poverty Nexus, p. 5) In their Concluding Observations, p. 18, they add, "The trickle down process of growth has been weak since growth is not located in sectors where labour is concentrated (for example, agriculture) and in states where poverty is concentrated (for example, Bihar, Orissa, Madhya Pradesh and Uttar Pradesh)". Their concern is that "The present pattern of growth has the potential for widening inequality" and "if inequality increases beyond a limit, social disarticulation would set in that may become a major barrier to growth".

[8] World Food Programme 2008, www.wfp.org.

[9] Food and Agriculture Organization, www.faostat.fao.org.

Gini coefficient of the distribution of adult schooling years in the population, a crude measure of educational inequality, was 0.56 in India in 1998–2000, which is not just higher than 0.37 in China in 2000, but even higher than almost all Latin American countries.[10]

When it comes to land distribution, Bardhan estimates the Gini coefficient of asset inequality in rural India at 0.62 in 2002 as against China's 0.49 in the same year.[11] It must be much worse in most other South Asian countries, particularly Pakistan, where hardly a beginning has been made in land reforms, and Nepal, where the Republican revolution has barely begun. This one factor also probably accounts for Bhutan's and Sri Lanka's disturbing ranking on the Gini index. (How much the fair distribution of land contributes to equality is made startlingly evident in the case of Ethiopia, one of the poorest low-HDI countries in the world but with a Gini index ranking comparable to the best: on par with the Czech Republic and not much below star performers like Norway!)[12]

In consequence, there is a deeply disturbing disjunction between rapid GDP growth and the slow pace of HDI amelioration (that is, the difference between the plus First-World consumption patterns of the privileged and the abysmal living conditions of the deprived which characterises and defines South Asia). While we are told that India under economic reforms has zoomed from the nadir of the "Hindu rate of growth"[13] to being today the second-fastest growing economy

---

[10] Bardhan, *supra*.

[11] Bardhan, *op. cit.*

[12] Ethiopia   29.8
     Czech/Norway   25.8

(UN HDR 2009, *op. cit.*, Table M)

[13] The fact is that in the first decade of planning, the Indian GDP growth rate was raised by as much as a factor of 5 over the growth rate bequeathed to us by British colonial rule. British India's average annual growth rates from 1914 to 1947 have been variously estimated by economists Angus Maddison, Alan Heston and Sivasubramonian at between 0.73 and 1.22 percent (Bipin Chandra, "The Colonial Legacy", in *The Indian Economy: Problems and Prospects,* ed. Bimal Jalan [New Delhi: Penguin, 1997], Table 4, p. 12). So, 3.5–4 percent represented an exponential leap in growth rates over the past and, therefore, was not to be denigrated.

in the world — second only, as in everything, to China! — what is mentioned only *sotto voce*, if it is bruited about at all, is that in the last 15 years, India has gone from the 134th position on the UN HDI to, well, the 134th position today. The fruits of accelerated growth have been so disproportionately distributed, so unfairly skewed, that whereas in terms of dollar billionaires in 2007–2008 we were rated fourth in the world in terms of numbers (and second in the world in terms of their collective assets),[14] the average Indian — the *aam aadmi* — stagnates in comparative terms exactly where he was an aeon ago.

Of course, in absolute numbers, and therefore in terms of HDI values, there has been improvement, for the report tells us India has moved up from an HDI value of 0.427 in 1980 to 0.511 in 1995 to 0.612 in 2007, thus raising the HDI value by 0.101 in the last 12 years compared to 0.084 in the previous 15 years, reflecting marginally higher average incomes across income categories, marginally increased spending and marginally better results in poverty alleviation.[15]

But one cannot help noting that over both the long-term period 1980–2007 and the medium-term period 1995–2007, there is an almost inverse relationship in South Asia between HDI ranking and

---

[14] P. Sainath, sourced from http//www.forbes.com/fdc/welcome_mjx.shtm and cited in a lecture to the Bureau of Parliamentary Studies and Training, New Delhi, 6 September 2007. The position has altered since last year's meltdown and is changing again with the present recovery.

[15] Extracted from Table G, "Human Development Index Trends", Human Development Report 2009, pp. 167–170:

	1980	1995	2007
India	0.427	0.511	0.612
Pakistan	0.402	0.469	0.572
Nepal	0.309	0.436	0.553
Bangladesh	0.328	0.415	0.543
Sri Lanka	0.649	0.696	0.759
Afghanistan	...	...	0.352
Maldives	...	...	0.771
China	0.533	0.657	0.772

improvement in HDI values: thus, Nepal and Bangladesh, at the lower end in HDI ranking, have registered long-term improvements of 0.244 and 0.215 in HDI values, and of 0.129 (Bangladesh) and 0.117 (Nepal) in the medium term, whereas India and Pakistan, ranked higher than Nepal and Bangladesh but well below Sri Lanka and the Maldives, have done less well than the lower ranked (long-term: 0.185 and 0.170, respectively, and medium-term: 0.101 and 0.103, respectively) but better than the higher-ranked Sri Lanka and the Maldives (0.063 and 0.088 respectively in the medium term and 0.110 in the long term — Sri Lanka only, as the Maldives figure is not available).[16]

The best argument for higher growth, even if it stretches inequality, is well illustrated by India's example of high GDP growth and lowered taxes having so swollen government revenues that government expenditure on anti-poverty programmes has risen exponentially (if in nominal terms) by an astonishing factor of 15 over the last 15 years — from central budget allocations of around Rs. 7500 crore in 1994–1995 to over Rs. 120,000 crore in 2008–2009 (further upped to Rs. 125,000 crore in the current fiscal year).[17]

Tragically — and this is the running theme of my argument — outlays have had no relationship with outcomes, outcomes having been nowhere near commensurate with dramatically increased outlays. Indeed, through the most accelerated phase of growth in India's economic history, which is the first decade of this century, we have actually slipped in our ranking on the UN HDI. Our relative position on the HDI has disturbingly deteriorated in conjunction with our rise

---

[16] Afghanistan is being excluded from this comparative analysis for obvious reasons of war-torn conditions and the absence of full statistical information. China's HDI value at 0.772 in 2007 is comparable to the Maldives (0.771) and Sri Lanka (0.759), but considerably above other South Asian countries: Bhutan (0.619), India (0.612), Pakistan (0.572), Nepal (0.553) and Bangladesh (0.543).

[17] At an exchange rate of Rs. 40 to the US dollar, this means the central government allocation for such programmes rose from USD 1875 million in 1994–1995 to over USD 30,000 million in 2008–2009, further upped to around USD 31,250 million in the current fiscal.

in GDP growth, as illustrated by our sinking from 126 to 128 to 132 to 134 over precisely the period of accelerating growth (2004–2007), even as, curiously, our worst performance in GDP growth since economic reforms (1997–2002) coincided with our rising on the UN HDI from 132 to 127![18]

Why are higher outlays impacting so relatively little on all that makes life more bearable for the poor? And why is political attention to the issues of poverty so muted in comparison to the hurrahs we hear over GDP growth rates?[19]

The gravamen of my paper is that the problem lies in the answer to the second question — the muted attention given to issues of poverty alleviation relative to the race for economic superpower status — even as the solution lies in the answer to the first question — why outcomes are non-commensurate with outlays.

---

[18] India's ranking on the UN HDI:

1997	132
1998	128
1999	115
2000	124
2001	127
2002	127
2003	127
2004	126
2005	128
2006	132
2007	134

(Compiled from successive UN HDI reports. It may be noted that the base year of the data is two years old. Thus, the report for 1999 will refer to the ranking in 1997 and the report for 2009 to the ranking in 2007. However, changes in the total numbers of countries surveyed and in methodology call for caution in comparing rankings over the years.)

[19] Cf. N.C.B. Nath, "Political Perspectives on Chronic Poverty" in *Chronic Poverty and Development Policy in India*, ed. A.K. Mehta and A. Shepherd (New Delhi: Sage, 2006), pp. 248–271: "… the political class is, by and large, not equipped or willing to deal with chronic poverty problems" (p. 266). See also Table 8.3 on pp. 258–259 which provides a useful compendium of Selected Opinions on Poverty Reduction and Political Regimes.

Let me outline the problem first before I move to the solution: The politics of our poverty is reflected in the poverty of our politics.

Even the concept of a single National Poverty Line is ethically, politically and economically flawed for not recognising either the various components of multiple, multidimensional deprivation — ranging from the geographic to the social to the intergenerational, or its "drivers", "maintainers" and "interrupters" — or the various categories of poverty, ranging from the "chronic poor" to the "severely poor" to the "moderately poor" to the "dynamics of poverty — movement into or out of poverty, or staying in it",[20] to which I would add the "transient poor" (as distinct from the "perennial poor", by which I mean those thrown out of employment after years of holding a steady job who tend to become, as in Gujarat, 2002, the vanguard of the "angry proletariat".

The National Commission for Enterprises in the Unorganised Sector has in its August 2007 Report on Conditions of Work and Promotion of Livelihoods in the Unorganised Sector identified the following categories of "poor", each of which requires an individually tailored strategy for poverty alleviation and eventual eradication: extremely poor; poor; marginally poor; and vulnerable. While the number of "extremely poor" and "poor" has decreased, in 2004–2005 they still comprised 237 million people; meanwhile the number of poor and vulnerable together numbered 836 million, or 77 percent of the population. Notwithstanding the rise in middle- and high-income persons to a significant 253 million, those crying out for help constitute three to four times the number who have succeeded in standing on their own feet.[21]

Instead of comprehending these complexities of multiple dimensions of poverty, the National Poverty Line divides the entire population into two comfortable categories — the BPL (Below Poverty Line, about Rs. 10 per day) and the Above Poverty Line (APL). This is "comfortable" for two reasons. First, poverty alleviation can then be reduced to the entirely feasible proposition of shifting some top-of-the-line BPL over the line into the APL category and calling it "poverty alleviation". Second, because it eliminates the tiresome distinction between the

---

[20] Mehta and Shepherd, *op. cit., Chronic Poverty in India: An Introduction*, pp. 23–52.
[21] Table 1.2, p. 6.

marginal survivor and the obscenely rich: all are APL and all, therefore, beneficiaries, in some aggregated manner, of the growth process.

Under the National Poverty Line, only 26 percent are considered "poor" whereas by any reasonable definition of poverty 77 percent at least ought to be regarded as "poor". That is why a nuanced, graded and multi-deprivational definition of "poverty" should be the starting point of any really serious frontal assault on poverty.

Alas, the poor are yet to find their voice, even as the media (for that matter, the entire establishment) have become the megaphone of the classes that are prospering. The preference for growth over social justice, indeed, the argument that economic growth *is* the road to social justice, is advocated — with considerable vigour, I might add — by the "dismal science of economics" on the classroom economics argument bluntly stated by Prof. Bardhan (even if he strongly disagrees with the argument) that: "Preoccupation with inequality is harmful even for the poor because more equity is achieved only at the expense of efficiency and economic growth".[22]

Governance in a time of rapid growth does indeed privilege growth over equity — and justifies such privileging on the irrefutable ground that as growth, and growth alone, provides the resources for the war on poverty, equity at the expense of growth leads only to the redistribution of poverty. Hence the mocking of the slogan which won Indira Gandhi an unbelievable two-thirds majority against all comers combined in the 1971 general elections: "*Woh kehte hain Indira hatao, hum kehte hain Garibi hatao*" ("They say: Remove Indira; We say: Remove Poverty").

The contemporary establishment view is that the promotion of prosperity for some, even if it means for the moment delaying distributive justice for most, should be encouraged if we are to redistribute prosperity rather than redistribute poverty. While, therefore, overcoming poverty remains the overarching goal of proclaimed economic policy, the sensible first principle of economic administration, it is said, ought to lie in avoiding sentimental slogan-mongering and recognising that widening disparities are an inevitable concomitant of higher growth, so that higher growth becomes the top priority for

---

[22] Bardhan, *supra*.

it will lead eventually to the redistribution of prosperity on a tide that lifts all boats (even if the rising tide merely laps at the low-lying boats while raising all yachts to tsunami heights!).[23]

I concede the validity of the argument that vastly augmented government revenues do indeed constitute the necessary precondition for mounting a battering of the citadel of poverty. Indian fiscal policy post-economic reforms has definitely demonstrated that higher growth combined with lower taxes so amazingly boosts government revenues that through the pumping of vast additional resources into the war on poverty, accelerated growth almost simultaneously translates into inclusive growth. Unfortunately, it does not:

If it did, the World Bank's growth indicators would be reflected in similar trends on the UN Human Development Index. As we have already seen, they are not; nor is there an identifiable gestation period over which the two tend to come into alignment.

In consequence, while there is no argument that augmented resources, of the kind generated by economic liberalisation, are the *necessary* condition for poverty alleviation, it is becoming increasingly evident in South Asia that exponential augmentation of anti-poverty spending is not the *sufficient* condition for even poverty alleviation, let alone poverty eradication.

In short, what, over and above increased spending, is required for accelerated growth to translate into inclusive growth? The answer, I fervently believe, lies in inclusive governance.

In the absence of inclusive governance, the people at the grassroots, that is, the intended beneficiaries of poverty alleviation programmes, are left abjectly dependent on a bureaucratic delivery mechanism over which they have no effective control. The alternative system would be participatory development, where the people themselves are enabled to build their own future through elected representatives responsible to the local community and, therefore, responsive to their needs.

---

[23] Sitaram Yechury has argued that "while the taxes foregone through subsidies to the corporates was Rs. 4,28,000 crore annually, the allocation for Public Distribution System was Rs. 52,489 crore", nine times less (*The Hindu*, 27 October 2009). It may be noted that Yechury is a top-ranking leader of the Communist Party of India (Marxist).

Not only is responsive bureaucratic administration almost a contradiction in terms, the Indian and South Asian experience of the last six decades would appear to confirm that bureaucratic delivery mechanisms absorb a disproportionately high share of the earmarked expenditure: up to 85 paise in the rupee, said Rajiv Gandhi; perhaps 83 paise, says the Planning Commission in a recent evaluation; not quite so high, says the Prime Minister. We can leave it to experts to argue how many angels can dance on the head of a pin; for our purposes, it is enough to note that 75–85 percent of expenditure on poverty alleviation schemes is absorbed by the delivery mechanism itself. No wonder outcomes are so derisory.

Worse, precisely because (in India) over a hundred schemes are delivered to the same set of beneficiaries through mutually insulated administrative silos, set up by central government ministries intent on jealously guarding their respective fiefdoms, convergence of schemes at the delivery point becomes virtually impossible, thus depriving beneficiaries of the multiplier effect that would operate if the beneficiaries themselves, through their locally elected leaders, were to have the authority to plan and implement the utilisation of these resources in keeping with their own respective priorities.

So far, I am on well-trodden ground. But the argument for a systemic reordering of the delivery mechanism to shift from bureaucratic delivery to participatory development runs much deeper. Let me elaborate.

In Nehruvian independent India, constitutional governance and parliamentary democracy, combined with the integration of the princely states and fairly far-reaching land reforms, led to a rapid dismantling of the dominant and crushing feudalism of the colonial and precolonial period, promoting the political and social *empowerment* of a rising middle class. That middle class quickly secured privileged access to their *entitlements*, particularly in the two key human development areas of education and health. From the earliest phases of planned development, the Nehruvian state furnished the very best of world-class education and technical training at perhaps the world's cheapest costs to the brightest in the middle class through good to very good to truly outstanding Central Universities, a network of Indian Institutes of Technology and Indian Institutes of Management, and a large number of excellent medical schools, including the famed All-India Institute of

Medical Sciences.[24] More recently, private engineering and technical training colleges, general educational institutions and schools of business, as well as private universities like Amity and private hospitals like Apollo and Max, have ensured a wide ambit of educational and health opportunities to those who can afford to pay for them. *Thus empowerment has led to entitlements.* And the combination of empowerment and entitlements has given India's middle class *enrichment* on a scale undreamt of a generation or two ago. This is what has made India such a fast- and high-rising star on the international economic stage. The sheer size of our middle class makes us, in absolute numbers, a huge market and a mouth-watering investment destination. Add to India two of the most populous nations of the world, Pakistan and Bangladesh, and two of the most resurgent ones, Nepal and Sri Lanka, and you can see what makes us South Asia Rising.[25]

But because the numbers of our desperately poor are much, very much larger, and their living conditions among the very worst in the world, and with the amelioration in their condition being so pathetically slow, I had earlier described the slogans of "India Shining" and "South Asia Rising" as "slightly bogus".

The challenge is to convert accelerated growth into inclusive growth — and the path favoured by government after government in

---

[24] It is the graduates of these institutions who are spearheading India's march to the vanguard in information technology and making the health services of the United Kingdom and the United States possible. It is also they who are providing the world with Indian expertise in entrepreneurship, business management, finance and banking. There is, however, a downside to the story. In a lecture at the FICCI auditorium, New Delhi, in the mid-1990s, which I cite from memory, Prof. Amartya Sen pointed out that while there were six times as many graduates and postgraduates that India was churning out every year than China, China, on the other hand, had six times as many as Indian children in primary school. That perhaps accounts for where China has soared and where India has gone wrong.

[25] Anil Kumar Jain and Parul Gupta, "Globalisation: The Indian Experience", *Mainstream*, 8–14 February 2008, show that the number of Indian billionaires rose from 9 in 2004 to 40 in 2007, with a combined wealth that increased in a single year, 2006–2007, from $106 billion to $170 billion, overtaking China and Japan that respectively had only 17 and 24 billionaires! We can be proud of this burgeoning entrepreneurship — or saddened by the gross inequalities it reveals.

India, and more generally in South Asia, has been to exponentially increase spending on anti-poverty programmes in the expectation that a critical mass of expenditure will somehow be reached for the money thrown at the poor to become the straw they can clutch at to rise out of their misery. The intention is sound but commentator after commentator rues the fact that implementation has been hopeless. But, as is the wont of economists as a tribe, they point the finger of accusation — dreadfully poor implementation — and then think it is someone else's job to find the solution.[26]

What then is the systemic solution? I suggest that it lies in replicating for the poor the same pattern that has brought such

---

[26] See, for example, *The India Mosaic* (New Delhi: Academic Foundation, 2004), edited for the Rajiv Gandhi Foundation by Bibek Debroy, who suggested my name for this Inaugural Address. His own contribution to the volume, "The Idea of India and the Economic Tryst", quotes Nehru's famous "Tryst with Destiny" speech: "The service of India means the service of the millions who suffer. It means the ending of poverty and ignorance and disease and inequality of opportunity", and then goes on to deplore, in much the same terms used here, how distant we are from that goal. But beyond saying "The national goal cannot be accepted as a national one without a buy-in by these deprived sections", there is little by way of a roadmap as to how this might be achieved.

Similarly, the eight-point programme for dealing with chronic poverty suggested by Mehta and Shepherd, *op. cit.*, pp. 46–48, includes a number of normative recommendations but not a word on governance issues.

Arjun Sengupta's *Reforms, Equity and the IMF* (New Delhi: Har-Anand, 2001), makes the case on pp. 255–256 that "Development, however, is not just a matter of increasing the GDP" and touches on the key point that "in social sector investments, there is so much fat and wastage that a proper system of delivering public expenditure through government organisations and Panchayats might have so much impact on productivity that it may not require much increase in the quantum of investment as against a properly targeted implementation of the existing investments themselves" — but does not elaborate, rather like Pontius Pilate who "would not wait for an answer"!

William N. Bissell, whose *Making India Work* (New Delhi: Penguin, 2009) is making waves, actually seeks to promote people's participation by dismantling Panchayat Raj (p. 200)!

Even the latest foray into this subject, *India: Perspectives on Equitable Development* (New Delhi: Academic Foundation, 2009), excellent in analysing the problem, falls short on the systemic solution.

impressive, growing and assured prosperity to our burgeoning middle classes: *empowerment* leading to *entitlements* and the two together to *enrichment*: E-E-E.

Not until the disadvantaged and the deprived are politically and socially empowered to build their own lives will they secure genuine and broad-spectrum access to their basic entitlements. In our experience of serving up their entitlements of primary education, minimum health facilities, the public distribution system and rural infrastructure through the district and sub-district level bureaucracy and technocracy has been the single biggest failure of governance at the grassroots. Patchy, sporadic access to entitlements in the absence of empowerment to secure entitlements is principally what has rendered outcomes so hopelessly out of alignment with outlays. It is only through empowerment and grassroots democracy that the poor will secure their entitlement to grassroots development and from there to enrichment for all.

It was such empowerment of the most discriminated against section of the most deprived segment of society — the poor rural woman — that informed the remarkable experiment in village banking that has led to the women's self-help group revolution all over South Asia sparked by Bangladesh Nobel Laureate Mohammad Younus' Grameen Bank movement.

In India, constitutionally sanctioned and sanctified Panchayat Raj; in Pakistan, the Nazim system of administration;[27] in Sri Lanka, President Rajapakse's plans of reinforcing provincial devolution by taking devolution down to the village unit;[28] in the Maldives, the recent decision to convert the Ministry of Atolls into a Ministry of Local Government; in Afghanistan, the major thrust being given to such devolution by the Karzai government through the Community Development Councils under the National Solidarity Programme and the setting up of an Independent Directorate of Local

---

[27] Kudos to Minister Daniyal Aziz who achieved more in a shorter time than any of his South Asian colleagues, including myself.

[28] Kudos to Minister Tissa Vitharana who is throwing himself into the exercise with vigour and dynamism.

Government;[29] and the ancient systems of village panchayats in Nepal and village autonomy in Bhutan — all indicate an awareness of the need to anchor village development in village empowerment.

Unfortunately, tragically I would say, the planning and implementation of anti-poverty and grassroots development programmes in all these countries remains self-defeatingly centralised, devolution being largely confined to good intentions and scraps of paper, lacking in political will and conviction at the higher echelons and compromised at the lower echelons by a petty bureaucracy loathe to cede its power and pelf to humble if elected village folk.

There are no managerial solutions to poverty alleviation. The colonial mindset has to be thoroughly rehauled to promote a massive systemic change that replaces the patronizing, slow-footed bureaucratic delivery mechanism with a system of local self-governance that vests social and political power in elected representatives at the local community level, representative of the community that elected them, responsible to their local electorate and, therefore, responsive to the needs, demands and priorities of their constituents. In India, Prime Minister Rajiv Gandhi rewrote the three Rs of learning — reading, 'riting and 'rithmetic — into the three Rs of democratic local self-government: *representation* fostering *responsibility* and responsibility leading to *responsiveness*[30]: R-R-R to realise E-E-E!

The key lies in scientific activity mapping based on the principle of subsidiarity — which holds that anything that can be done at the lower level should be done at that level and no higher level — such that carefully and consensually structured activity maps detail the *functions* to be devolved respectively to the village, intermediate and district levels, and thus provide the basis on which the devolution of *finances* is to be patterned, matched by a parallel devolution of

---

[29] Kudos to M. Ehsan Zia, Minister of Rural Rehabilitation and Development, as well as IDLG Director, Jilani Popal, two extraordinarily sincere individuals dedicated to devolution in the most exacting of political circumstances.

[30] Rajiv Gandhi, *Selected Speeches and Writings 1988* (New Delhi: Publications Division, 1989) p. 164, address to District Magistrates at Jaipur, 30 April 1988: "our basic equation, namely, that Representativeness and Responsibility equal Responsiveness".

functionaries to each level of self-governance, in rural as much as in urban localities. Three Fs — functions, finances and functionaries — to provide the framework for the three Rs to lead us down the three-fold E-E-E path! Simple, no?

Such empowerment will enable the local community to deploy the financial resources made available to them and mobilised by them to plan and implement their own programmes of grassroots development and poverty eradication instead of depending on the grudging patronage of higher-level politicians, who have their own agenda, and an indifferent, self-serving local bureaucracy: grassroots development through grassroots democracy. This is what I call inclusive governance. And as Prime Minister Dr. Manmohan Singh said on 16 January 2009, there can be no inclusive growth without inclusive governance.

In India, we are already deep into the world's greatest experiment in democracy — 250,000 elected institutions of local self-government to which our people have elected 3.2 million representatives, with proportional representation at each level for the scheduled castes and scheduled tribes, a special legal dispensation for tribal areas, and, most important, 1.2 million elected women representatives drawn from every economic class and every social segment: gender empowerment on a scale without precedent in history or parallel in the world. There are more elected women in India alone than in the rest of the world put together. If only the UNDP would factor in elected women local government representatives, instead of limiting itself to women elected to the legislatures, India would be much higher on the UN Gender Equality Index, and therefore the HDI, than it is at present. Pakistan also has a huge host of elected women representatives at the grassroots. It is to be hoped — indeed, expected — that other countries of South Asia will follow suit as they take democracy down to the grassroots.

Unfortunately, even in India, while the institutions of local self-governance are in place, their contribution to grassroots development has been negligible on account of a virtual failure of political will and an absence of recognition in finance ministries and planning commissions of the nuances of devolution, reflected in inadequate and unscientific activity mapping. Painfully slow and grossly uneven progress on the devolution of the three Fs has made the three Rs virtually non-functional. In consequence, the journey to the three Es has barely begun even 16 years after the required constitutional amendments were enacted.

There lies the fundamental explanation for India's shameful showing on the UN's Human Development Index contrasted with her spectacular showing on GDP and GDP-related indices. The imperative of inclusive growth has been grasped, but the imperative of inclusive governance has been barely comprehended notwithstanding the Prime Minister's public endorsement of the centrality of inclusive governance to inclusive growth. The story is perhaps a little better, but not much, both in Pakistan and Bangladesh. And, as already indicated, we are still at the rudimentary beginnings of institution-building for inclusive governance in the other South Asian countries.

Not until the Ministry of Panchayat Raj becomes as central to the development process as the Ministry of Finance and the Planning Commission will accelerated growth start manifesting itself as inclusive growth. The same holds true of Ministries of Local Self-Government, by whatever name called or still to be called, in our South Asian neighbours.

Let me go even further. Not till we have a Ministry of Poverty Alleviation which incorporates a Department of Panchayat Raj will we find our way to inclusive growth through inclusive governance. For departmental programmes of accelerated growth are so exclusive of inclusive governance provisions and so innocent of any understanding of the nature, gradations and dimensions of poverty or of any impact assessment on poverty, inequality and human development of their policy proposals that the accelerated growth process initiated by economic reforms has often been at the expense of inclusive growth.[31] We see this in the virtual drying up of public capital formation in

---

[31] Amit Bhaduri, "Predatory Growth", *Economic and Political Weekly*, 19 April 2008, which points to "the mechanism by which growing inequality drives growth and growth fuels further inequality".

agriculture and allied activities, resulting in an agrarian crisis of almost 1960s proportions staring down at us two decades into economic reforms;[32] we find this reflected in the need to cap the fiscal deficit by restricting public investment to open the space for private sector capital mobilisation;[33] we see it too in growing unemployment fostered by capital-intensive industrialisation;[34] and we see it in rapidly falling employment in what till the 1980s was one of the largest employers, especially of the poor, in the Indian economy, the hand-looms sector.[35] Heartbreakingly, nearly two decades after the Constitution was amended, almost all Central Sector Schemes give

---

[32] D. Narasimha Reddy and Srijit Mishra in *India Development Report 2008*, *op. cit.*, trace "the present all pervading crisis in Indian agriculture" to "the severity of impact of economic reforms on rural India" where liberalisation of the internal market and the external trade sector has combined with fiscal reforms which have had "grave implications for public investment in agriculture and rural infrastructure" (Table 3.1). In consequence, "Gross Capital Formation in Indian agriculture declined drasti-cally...to one-third in 1999–2000 of the level in 1980–1981" (p. 44) in contrast with "the post-Independence period where the state had a dominant protective as well as promotional role" (p. 40). Therefore, "the farming community is passing through a particularly high stress situation during this high growth reform period" (p. 49).

[33] Bhaduri, *op. cit.*: "Inequality and distress grows as the state rolls back public expen-diture in social services like basic health, education and public distribution and neg-lects the poor, while the discipline imposed by the financial markets serves the rich and the corporations...That is the reason why successive Indian governments have willingly accepted the Fiscal Responsibility and Budget Management Act (2003) restricting deficit spending" — until the latest crisis in financial markets, I might add!

[34] *Ibid*: "productivity growth comes from mechanisation and longer hours of work". At the Jamshedpur steel plant, "output increased approximately by a factor of five, employment dropped by a factor of half, implying an increase in labour productivity by a factor of 10". At the Bajaj motorcycle factory in Pune, "more than double the output (was secured) with less than half the labour force, an increase in labour pro-ductivity by a factor of nearly six". In consequence, while in "earlier times", "4 percent growth on an average was associated with 2 percent growth in employment, India is experiencing a growth rate of some 7–8 percent in recent years, but the growth in regular employment has hardly exceeded 1 percent".

[35] *Examining Employment Figures in the Handloom Sector* (NCAER, 2006) estimates a drop in employment from the 1980s of over 4 million to around 2 million now (a third of the official figure). The study was commissioned by the All India Artisans and Craftworkers Welfare Association.

Panchayat Raj short shrift, preferring to rely on their own separate bureaucratic delivery mechanisms, with NGO rather than local participation. Each of these points warrants a separate lecture and I would suggest collaborative research on these points between ISAS and Indian and other South Asian academics, specifically into the point made by Mehta and Shepherd:

> ...the chronic poor have a right to benefit from growth and development. The unacceptably high levels of poverty and hunger that persist reflect the denial of this right...if the poverty of the poorest is not addressed sooner rather than later, it may become more intractable and costly later.[36]

Much of the dichotomy between growth and equity arises through the privileging of accelerated growth over inclusive growth.[37] None of this can be rectified where it matters most — at the grassroots — without inclusive governance reprioritising public investment decisions that, through inclusive governance by representative institutions of local self-governance, foster patterns of inclusive growth. Although I am talking of India, I believe these fundamental truths apply as much, and perhaps even more, to the other South Asian countries — more because their systems of local self-governance are even less developed than India's.

I wish GDP growth rates were all that there is to predicting the socio-economic outlook for my country and the countries of our neighbourhood. Sadly, the UN Human Development Report comes as a damper, a reality check on how far my country, in particular, and

---

[36] *Op. cit.*, pp. 23–24.

[37] P. Sainath, *The Hindu*, 15 August 2009, on tax revenues foregone in the interests of reviving GDP growth rates: "Simply put, the corporate world has grabbed concessions in just two years (2008–2009 and 2009–2010) that total more than seven times the 'fiscally imprudent' farm loan waiver. In fact, it means that on average we have been feeding the corporate world close to Rs. 700 crore every day in these two years". The calculation is based on concessions in direct taxes alone and does not include tax revenues foregone in indirect taxation.

the South Asian region, in general, have to go before we can lay any claim to being, in moral or human terms, even a just country, let alone a humane nation dedicated to Mahatma Gandhi's goal of "wiping every tear from every eye".

It is a dangerous delusion to imagine that prosperity for a sliver of our population — even if that sliver runs to hundreds of millions in absolute numbers — can blind us to the reality of a billion and many hundreds of millions more living in dreadful, dreary poverty with little to indicate that within any acceptable period of time they will secure even a modicum of a fair share of our accelerated growth to relieve the daily drudgery of their lives. We need Shining Indians and Rising South Asians more than Shining India or Rising South Asia. And we can get them by listening to Mahatma Gandhi responding on the eve of our Independence to a question about the "India of your dreams". The Mahatma replied: "I shall work for an India in which the poorest shall feel that it is their country, in whose making they have an effective voice".[38]

Let us give our people an "effective voice" in the making of our countries.

---

[38] But the Karnataka poet, Gita Mahadeva Prasad, has perhaps said the last word:

"Dear Gandhi,
On the wall
We have framed you.
See how the frames
Struggle to
Keep you in place!" (*The Interior*, Bangalore: Karthik Prakashana, undated, probably 2009)

Chapter 4

Political Developments in South Asia: Issues and Outlook[1]

Sartaj Aziz

As many are aware, South Asia has been the centre of several ancient civilisations. It shares a rich heritage and culture. It is endowed with vast natural and human resources. The people of the region are talented and industrious. Yet it has fallen behind in the development race. In the past three decades many countries of East Asia and Southeast Asia have reformed their economies, attracted huge foreign investment, accelerated their growth rates and transformed the lives of their people. In comparison, as Mani Shankar Aiyar described so eloquently, poverty, hunger, disease and illiteracy continue to stalk the lands of South Asia. About 40 percent of the total population in South Asia is still living below the poverty line of one dollar a day. The misery of the poor people is further enhanced by religious, ethnic or gender discrimination and repression of one kind or another. The underlying causes are political.

South Asia has also become a melting pot of several global fault-lines. The growth of extremism and Islamic fundamentalism in Afghanistan and their spillover into Pakistan, for example, are a direct legacy of the proxy war between the USSR and the USA, which started with the Russian invasion of Afghanistan. The tragic events of September 11, 2001, and the invasion of Afghanistan in October 2001, have set into motion another chain of events in the

---

[1] This is an edited version of the paper presented at the 5th International Conference on South Asia organized by the Institute of South Asian Studies, University of Singapore, on 4 November 2009.

region, whose ultimate consequences are difficult to predict at this stage.

Apart from the continuing India–Pakistan tensions over the long-standing Kashmir dispute, there are high-intensity conflicts within most countries of South Asia. These include the prolonged conflict with the Tamil Tiger movement in Sri Lanka, the Maoist movement in Nepal, sectarian and ethnic tensions in Pakistan, insurgency in the North East and periodical communal tensions in India. These conflicts, which highlight the structural problems inherent in heterogeneous societies, are serious obstacles to the establishment of sustainable political systems and viable institutions of good governance and inclusive governance.

The challenge before the leaders and policy makers of South Asia is whether or not they can overcome these obstacles and grasp the opportunities for economic and social progress that lie ahead.

By including this session on political development under the theme "Beyond the Global Financial Crisis", the organisers of the conference have recognised the importance of political stability in reviving economic growth and overcoming the crisis.

Positive Political Developments

There are many positive elements in the present political landscape of South Asia. In fact, the years 2008–2009 will go down in the history of South Asia as a milestone because in these 18 months democracy has returned to three important countries of South Asia.

- Pakistan had its general elections in February 2008, and despite many difficulties inherited from nine years of military rule, the main political parties of the country, the Pakistan People's Party and the Pakistan Muslim League (N), are working together to strengthen democratic institutions and traditions. The coalition of religious parties (MMA) which had won 61 out of 342 seats in the 2002 elections was able to win only 7 seats in 2008.
- Nepal, after a decade-long civil war and two years of uncertainty, elected a new Constituent Assembly in April 2008, with the

Maoists emerging as the largest party — 220 out of 601 seats. The new Assembly has abolished the monarchy and declared Nepal a republic. Progress in framing a new constitution has however proved more difficult. After only eight months in office, in May 2009, Maoist Prime Minister Prachanda resigned over the sacking of the Army Chief and Madhav Kumar Nepal of the United Marxist–Leninist Party (UML) emerged as the new Prime Minister with a loose alliance of 22 parties. The Constituent Assembly is still deadlocked but the coalition government was able to pass the annual budget in June 2009.

- The elections held in Bangladesh in January 2009 after two years of military-dominated caretaker setup, led by a technocrat, Mr. Fakhruddin Ahmed, were also quite remarkable. The efforts of the Army to create a third political force to overcome the persistent confrontation between the two mainstream parties, the Awami League and the Bangladesh Nationalist Party, did not succeed. The success of the Awami League led by Hasina Wajid was truly stunning. It won 230 or 77 percent of 300 seats in the Assembly, with rival BNP of Khalida Zia securing only 29 seats. The remaining 41 seats went to General Ershad's Jatiya Party and the Jamaat-e-Islami. The electorate, which voted against corruption and for Hasina Wajid and the BD Army that provided a level playing field, would now expect that she would fulfill her election promises and keep herself and her party free from corruption.

The Indian elections of April 2009 also produced a decisive victory for the Congress party and facilitated the establishment of a more stable coalition under Prime Minister Manmohan Singh. These elections with 420 million voters were the largest ever and were very well managed as Minister Shanmugam highlighted in his inaugural address. Indian voters apparently voted for economic development rather than the Bharatiya Janata Party's communal politics. If Manmohan Singh succeeds in implementing his campaign promises to expand programmes that directly impact the poor, it will not only transform India's "development model" but also influence development thinking in South Asia as a whole.

In May 2009, the two-decade-long war between the Sri Lankan army and the Tamil Tigers finally ended when Mahinda Rajapaksa, the President of Sri Lanka, declared on television that the military had won the final victory against the LTTE. There was international criticism about the large-scale killing and about the re-settlement of "war refugees" but the return of peace has improved opportunities for political reconciliation and faster economic growth in Sri Lanka in the coming years.

Another encouraging feature of South Asia is the emergence of a vibrant civil society in almost all South Asian countries in the past two decades. This is an essential prerequisite not only for evolving a viable democratic system but also for promoting more positive interactions among countries of South Asia.

Obstacles and Constraints

The most important flashpoint in South Asia at present is Afghanistan. As most of you are aware, the tragic events of 9/11 have cast long shadows on Asia, leading to devastating attacks on Iraq and Afghanistan. The Taliban fighters in Afghanistan melted away, in the face of the incessant bombardment in October 2001. Some took refuge in the eastern districts in Afghanistan and some crossed over into the tribal belt between Pakistan and Afghanistan. Then having regrouped in South Waziristan, foreign Taliban fighters joined hands with the so-called Pakistani Taliban, i.e. those associated with madrassahs in which they were trained for the war against Russia with support from the USA, and started extending their influence to other parts of the tribal areas and some adjoining districts. At the same time, the Afghan Taliban acquired more sophisticated weapons and have re-emerged as a formidable fighting force in Afghanistan. The US and its allies are also losing the battle for the hearts and minds of people partly because of widespread corruption and abuse of power by the Karzai government and partly because the post-2001 administration and its expanding army which is dominated by non-Pashtuns, i.e. Tajiks, Uzbeks and Hazaras. This has especially alienated the people of eastern and southern Afghanistan who are mostly Pashtuns.

In his report of August 2009, General Stanley McChrystal warned about the growing insurgency in Afghanistan, underlined a litany of mistakes that have been made and warned that the war in Afghanistan was not going well. President Obama is now considering General McChrystal's request for 40,000 additional troops, at a time when public support for continuing the war in Afghanistan has been on the decline.

In May 2009, the Pakistan government finally recognised that the threat of extremism from within Pakistan was greater than that posed by its hostile neighbour. The Pakistan Army launched a decisive operation to chase out militants from Malakand and adjoining areas. This operation, which was supported by all major political parties inside and outside the Parliament, was highly successful, even though it displaced over two million families for three to four months. In October 2009, the Army started the second phase of this operation by sending at least three divisions to South Waziristan where the local militants and their foreign supporters had established their training and communication infrastructure since 2003–2004. This is a more difficult terrain and the resistance is expected to be much stronger but, so far, the operation is going well. In retaliation, the extremists, with the support of jihadi organisations in the urban areas of the country, have unleashed a vicious string of suicide attacks and bomb blasts on military and police installations and in crowded markets. The month of October saw more terrorist activities than any other period in Pakistan's history: at least 300 killed in more than 20 attacks in different parts of the country and twice as many wounded. Two suicide attacks on the International Islamic University on 17 October, killing seven students, led to the closure of all educational institutions in the country for two weeks.

This new kind of war that has erupted in Pakistan will take time but the shift of policy, reflecting the resolve of the nation to carry this war to the finish, is a very significant development not just for Pakistan but for South Asia because the rise of extremism and militancy is a common problem for the countries of South Asia and, therefore, requires a concerted regional solution.

The second major negative political development has been the derailment of the peace process between India and Pakistan after the

November 2008 terrorist attacks in Bombay. The incident provoked
a traumatic reaction among the Indian public and the government of
India responded by suspending the composite dialogue and
announced that unless Pakistan punished the perpetrators of this
heinous crime, they would not resume dialogue. A cold war environment has prevailed ever since.

Another major challenge of a continuing nature for South Asian
countries is what might be called the crisis of governance. In all South
Asian countries this crisis, which has longer-term implications for
stability and progress, is reflected in large-scale poverty, growing
inequalities and unending exploitation of deprived communities:

- At least 500 million or one-third of the South Asian population
  live in dire poverty. Three-fourths of these poor people are in
  rural areas of South Asia. The urban poor also live in miserable
  conditions in shanty towns and slums, without access to clean
  drinking water or sanitation.
- Growing inequalities, resulting from unbalanced growth, have
  further compounded the inherited heterogeneity of South Asia in
  terms of religion, caste, ethnicity and culture. This, in turn, has
  accentuated social tensions leading to different types of local and
  regional conflicts. According to a recent World Bank study, South
  Asia has the world's largest conflict-affected population — about
  70 million.
- Despite many successful examples of improved public services and
  civil society initiatives, like the Grameen Bank, there are glaring
  inequalities in access to public goods and services. The most
  important of these services, not widely available to the poorer and
  weaker members of society, are speedy and inexpensive justice and
  accurate property records. Land mafias and municipal officials
  continue to exploit poor dwellers in shanty towns and female
  members of families seldom get their due share of the property.
- Poverty occurs when a household with no or limited assets is
  locked into a nexus of power which deprives the poor of their
  actual or potential income. The poor face markets, institutions
  and local power structures which discriminate against their access

to resources, public services and governance decisions that affect their immediate existence.

- Many political and social problems facing South Asia, including the spread of extremism and religious violence, can be traced directly to poverty, exploitation and poor governance.

This is a brief account of political developments in South Asia — the good news and the problems, some long-term and structural and some caused by external factors. But what is the outlook for the future?

Future Outlook

I hope most of you will agree that the countries of South Asia are truly at historic crossroads. They can either remain under the heavy burden of their chequered history, overwhelmed by their interstate and intrastate conflicts and, therefore, unable to lift the population from poverty and deprivation. Or they can learn to live and work together and take full advantage of the vast opportunities for development, trade and cooperation that are opening up. To follow the latter course will require a paradigm shift in the thinking, mindsets and policies of not only the leaders of South Asia, but all other stakeholders including their military and civilian establishments, their think tanks and their bureaucracies. Some illustrative suggestions:

- First, South Asian leaders have to make a deliberate and sustained effort to block out the negative fallout of global fault lines that have been sneaking into South Asia in different forms. The global players often attempt to shift the blame of their follies without any justification. For example, it is difficult to assess the potential threat to US security if it had not attacked Afghanistan after 9/11. But the attack has created actual and not potential dangers to Pakistan's security on a horrendous scale. The USA is now realising that Al-Qaeda in Afghanistan has no capability to harm the USA and hardly any Afghan has ever been involved in acts of terrorism in Europe or the USA. The Afghan Taliban are actually fighting against foreign occupation, as they did against the British in the 19th century and against Russia in 1980–1990. Pakistan did not face any insurgency on its western border prior to 2001. If countries of South Asia look at Afghanistan from this perspective, their policies can be readily reoriented in favour of South Asia rather than external powers that may have different agendas.

- Second, short-term political objectives must be relegated in favour of longer-term objectives. For example, the current Indian policy of keeping Pakistan on the defensive over the peace process may bring short-term gains in electoral politics, or keeping up pressures on jihadi organisations that were active in Kashmir in the past, but the long-term economic interests of India will not be well-served by the current state of tensions and political standoff between India and Pakistan. Dialogue must continue between the two countries even if there is no immediate outcome.

- Third, South Asia has to revive the vision of regional cooperation and intensify its efforts. The founding fathers of the South Asian Association for Regional Cooperation (SAARC) were obviously conscious of the paramount need for regional cooperation, to accelerate the pace of economic and social progress in South Asia, to overcome common problems and learn from each other's experience. They were also aware that the world trading system was dominated by three major trading blocs — Europe, the USA and Japan — with much greater access to world capital markets and capacity for research and development. Despite efforts to liberalise world trade under an open global trading system, they were following many protectionist and inward-looking policies that discriminated against developing countries, as Prof. Nachane pointed out this morning. In this situation, it was very evident that no single country could, by acting alone, improve its competitive position in the face of these inward-looking trading blocs. The decision to form SAARC in 1985 was therefore both timely and wise.

But unfortunately, after 24 years, SAARC has yet to achieve the noble vision of its founding fathers. In fact, very little progress has been made towards realising the practical goals envisaged for the Association in the economic, social or technological spheres. Grandiose plans and lofty rhetoric has usually taken the place of concrete and substantive cooperation. As the Group of Eminent Persons, which carried out the first independent appraisal of SAARC in 1998, had pointed out, SAARC has passed through two distinct phases. The first was the preparatory phase, in which certain non-controversial initiatives were taken in peripheral areas to build confidence and create the minimum necessary institutional mechanism. In the second half of its evolution, SAARC moved into its expansionary phase, when regional cooperation was expanded both in the social and core economic sectors. Many major commitments with far-reaching implications for the region were undertaken, including the SAARC Preferential Trading Arrangement (SAPTA). However, the member states did not vest in SAARC either adequate political will or sufficient resources for carrying out these commitments.

In January 2004, another landmark agreement was signed at the SAARC summit in Islamabad to move beyond SAPTA towards SAFTA or the South Asian Free Trade Area, under which tariffs were to be virtually abolished by 2013. The agreement was formally launched on 1 July 2006 but there has been only limited progress so far. The suspension of the India–Pakistan dialogue in December 2008 further slowed down the implementation of this Agreement. SAFTA must be put back on its scheduled track as soon as possible.

- Fourth, South Asia has to make systematic efforts to develop stronger economic, trade, financial and transport links with the rest of Asia, especially China and Japan. This will not only protect South Asia from the adverse consequences of periodical crises in the global financial markets dominated by the USA and Europe but also expand opportunities for trade and investment. In this context, the debate about building India as a counterweight to China's emergence as a regional power is, in my view, out-of-date. The future of both India and China lies in mutual cooperation as an important dimension of the rise of Asia. As Dr. Palit pointed out this morning, over 50 percent of Indian exports go to other

Asian countries. Asia has also been the cradle for many old civilisations, starting with the Mesopotamian civilisation to various Chinese dynasties and the ancient Indus Valley Civilisation. Despite the prolonged exploitation by colonial powers between the 16th and 20th centuries, Asia has retained its rich cultural and social heritage, which itself will be a great source of vitality in the future.

The prediction that the 21st century belongs to Asia is now universally accepted. The economic progress of Asia in the past three decades is based on solid foundations of education, science and technology. This has helped countries upgrade industrial structures and move into many hi-tech knowledge-based sectors like information and communication technologies. This factor will be decisive for Asia's capacity to compete with other countries in the open markets created by the process of globalisation.

Within Asia, South Asia is an important subcontinent with a combined population of 1.5 billion. It has the largest proportion of population below 15. Most of the educated young men and women can enter the job market with new skills, provided South Asia can integrate more closely with the dynamic economies of the rest of Asia.

Let me conclude by reproducing a quotation from a recent *New York Times* article by Yukio Hatoyama, then leader of the Democratic Party of Japan and now the Prime Minister of Japan:

> The Japan–US security pact will continue to be the cornerstone of Japanese diplomatic policy. But at the same time, we must not forget our identity as a nation located in Asia. I believe that the East Asian region, which is showing increasing vitality, must be recognized as Japan's basic sphere of being. So we must continue to build frameworks for stable economic cooperation and security across the region.
>
> The financial crisis has suggested to many that the era of US unilateralism may come to an end. It has also raised doubts about the permanence of the dollar as the key global currency. I also feel that as a result of the failure of the Iraq war and the financial crisis,

the era of US-led globalism is coming to an end and that we are moving towards an era of multipolarity.

The message, ladies and gentlemen, is loud and clear, if we care to listen and absorb. The rise of Asia is not stoppable. Let us start talking about an Asian common market and a common Asian currency.

Chapter 5

The Major Powers and Conflicts in South Asia

T.V. Paul

Introduction

The peace and conflict patterns of a given region are often significantly affected by the interactions and interventions of great powers in that region. The extent of such interventions depends heavily
on how the region measures in the strategic calculations of major
powers. If a region has high geostrategic salience for the major
powers' security and/or economic interests, it is likely to attract
the maximum attention of these powers. If major powers are in
conflict at the global level, they could bring that conflict to the
region by engaging in proxy wars and military alignments with
regional states. Regions that have high levels of enduring rivalries
also attract major power attention over concerns of stability or particular interests they generate for the powers' security and economic calculations.[1] Furthermore, regions where states are weak in
terms of their institutional and political capacity can be tempting
targets for major power intervention, especially if they generate
security challenges to regional and global orders. Major powers by
definition are states with global power capabilities, global security

---

[1] Enduring rivalries are defined as persistent or intractable conflicts with periodic mil-
itarised crises and wars. For more on these, see Paul Diehl and Gary Goertz, *War and
Peace in International Rivalry* (Ann Arbor: University of Michigan Press, 2001);
T. V. Paul, ed., *The India–Pakistan Conflict: An Enduring Rivalry* (Cambridge:
Cambridge University Press, 2005).

and economic interests and the ability to intervene beyond their immediate regional space. Despite these global interests, major powers need not be sufficiently cognisant of the particular regional contexts or sensitivities of the states and people concerned in their policy formulation and implementation.

The interactions of major powers and regional states often create systemic interdependencies and security complexes. While the larger international system is defined in terms of the interactions among major powers, a regional sub-system can similarly be defined in terms of the interactions among the key states of that region and the major power actors heavily involved in regional affairs.[2] This characterisation of a regional sub-system moves away from geographical and cultural proximities and may suffer from measurement problems beyond the strategic arena.

In a more specific sense, major powers can intervene in a region through competition, cooperation, engagement, disengagement, hegemony, or a mixture of these ideal types.[3] *Competitive* patterns suggest great powers bringing their outside conflict into the region and enrolling regional states in their mutual struggles. *Cooperation*, on the other hand, points to great powers avoiding competitive entanglements in the region while trying to solve conflicts among the regional states through institutional and/or diplomatic mechanisms. They may act as umpires or mediators among the regional powers during the latter's peace negotiations. *Engagement* may occur in a benign manner as major powers try to deal with regional states without taking into account their mutual conflict as the sole barometer of involvement. *Disengagement* would mean withdrawal after a period of

---

[2] David A. Lake, "Regional Security Complexes: A Systems Approach", in *Regional Orders*, ed. David A. Lake and Patrick M. Morgan (University Park, PA: Pennsylvania State University Press, 1997); Barry Buzan, "A Framework for Regional Security Analysis", in *South Asian Insecurity and the Great Powers*, ed. Barry Buzan and Gowher Rizvi (Houndmills: Macmillan, 1986), p. 8; Barry Buzan and Ole Weaver, *Regions and Powers: The Structure of International Security* (Cambridge: Cambridge University Press, 2004).

[3] Benjamin Miller, *States, Nations and the Great Powers: The Sources of Regional War and Peace* (Cambridge: Cambridge University Press, 2007), pp. 284–292.

competition or deep engagement. Finally, *hegemony* would imply that the major power simply dominates the region's security and economic architecture through its overwhelming preponderance in capabilities, economic presence and diplomatic power. The regional states, although juridically sovereign and independent, are constrained heavily by the whims of the major power or powers in undertaking particular actions, especially those affecting the security calculations of the hegemon. Through these mechanisms, major powers can affect the conflict and cooperation patterns in a region. As Benjamin Miller contends, major powers can influence a region's conflict pattern, transforming it from cold war to hot war or cold peace to warm peace and vice versa.[4] This does not imply that regional powers are often passive objects of major power activism. Through a variety of asymmetric means, regional powers can manipulate major powers and engage in regional affairs often benefitting the regional state's or state elite's interests. Israel and Pakistan typify these smaller powers with a history of successfully influencing their major power patrons.[5] However, from a deeper strategic and long-term point of view, such limited successes for the regional power may not indicate much about the chance for peace or war in a region or the economic and political development of the smaller state itself.

A region with multiple weak states and with geostrategic significance is ripe for major power activism. The weakness of these states is often caused by the incongruence between the formal juridical state and the nations or nationalities that comprise them. If several nations exist within a state and they are unwilling to give full allegiance to the state, a weak state is very likely to be formed. A weak state is one in which the state has serious capacity deficiencies in dealing with its multi-faceted problems, especially in the security area. In a previous work, I defined state capacity as "the ability of a state to develop and implement policies in order to provide collective goods such as security, order and welfare to its citizens in a legitimate and effective

---

[4] *Ibid.*

[5] Robert O. Keohane, "The Big Influence of Small Allies", *Foreign Policy*, 2 (Spring 1971): 161–182.

manner untrammeled by internal or external actors".[6] This definition goes beyond the Weberian approach equating a coercive state with a strong state, by including welfare and legitimacy factors in determining state capacity. Unlike in the past, in the contemporary world a proper democratic system may be essential for a state to obtain sufficient legitimacy internally and externally. In this conception, a strong state is one with not only the ability to engage in autonomous behavior but also legitimate behavior in the eyes of its citizens and the international community. At the most general level, a weak state is a state low in capacity, defined in terms of its ability to carry out its objectives with adequate societal support.[7] Since this definition draws together characteristics of the state apparatus itself and its relationship with societal actors, scholars have identified many different phenomena that indicate the general concept of capacity. According to Robert Rotberg, a weak state suffers from deficiencies in the areas of: (a) security (i.e. the state security forces, both military and police, are unable to provide basic security to all citizens in a legitimate and effective manner); (b) participation (open participation is limited as elections, if they take place at all, may not be fair and impartial); and (c) infrastructure (the physical infrastructure of the state is in very poor condition with health and literacy accorded low levels of national priority).[8] Major powers cannot resolve the problem of nation-to-state incongruence, but they can, through their support or absence of support, generate conditions for conflict to persist or dissipate over time.[9]

South Asia as a region has several of the above-mentioned characteristics and hence attracts a fair amount of major power activism.

---

[6] T.V. Paul, "State Capacity and South Asia's Perennial Insecurity Problems", in *South Asia's Weak States: Understanding the Regional Insecurity Predicament*, ed. T. V. Paul (Stanford: Stanford University Press, Forthcoming, 2010), Ch. 1.

[7] Eric A. Nordlinger, "Taking the State Seriously", in *Understanding Political Development: An Analytical Framework*, ed. Myron Weiner and Samuel P. Huntington (Boston: Little Brown, 1987), p. 369.

[8] Robert I. Rotberg, ed., *State Failure and State Weakness in a Time of Terror* (Washington, DC: Brookings Institution Press, 2003).

[9] Miller, *States, Nations*, pp. 62–81.

This region is geostrategically important for the major powers, and is simultaneously populated by weak states, except for the strong–weak state, India. However, over the years, India as a rising power with several major power attributes and aspirations has attracted engagement or limited containment/balancing by other major powers. This dual characteristic of the region generates much major power interest, although that attention has waxed and waned over the past 60 years of state formation and consolidation in South Asia.

South Asia and the Major Powers

The major powers play an important role in South Asia, despite India's dominant power position in the region. The region's pivotal geostrategic location is part of the reason for this; however, the presence of weak states in intense conflict and the existence of enduring rivalries contribute to this activism by outside powers, as in the cases of Afghanistan and Pakistan. The relatively high geostrategic salience of the region is also a function of its proximity to two other strategically important regions — the Middle East/Persian Gulf and East Asia. A large share of the world's oil supply flows through the Arabian Sea/Indian Ocean and the major power naval presence (especially American) has been pivotal for their strategic engagements in the Gulf region. The presence of multiple weak states which have not resolved the state-to-nation imbalance in an amicable manner also offers fertile grounds for major power activism in South Asia. These imbalances cause considerable amounts of irredentism among the pivotal states of the region. Often these irredentist struggles, led by ethnic groups and their insurgent forces living on both sides of the common borders of the states, are supported by sympathetic states and their officials. The tendency among South Asian states to intervene in the internal affairs of each other also provides opportunity for major powers to offer support or opposition to particular territorial or political claims.

Historically, systemic conflicts involving major power blocs have been important sources of great power activism in South Asia. Since the 1800s, the British–Russian, British–Japanese and US–Soviet rivalries were played out in some fashion in the region. The Cold War was the most intense systemic rivalry that has impinged on the security of the region in modern times. Both India and Pakistan were targets, as well as often willing partners, in the Cold War competition between the United States and the Soviet Union. Pakistan was a willing accomplice in the US-led alliance system, and it developed a strong military relationship with Washington that has witnessed several ups and downs since 1954. Pakistan's membership in US-led Cold War alliances, SEATO and CENTO in the 1950s, was a critical turning point for South Asia's strategic trajectory. Moreover, Pakistan allowed US spy planes to operate from its soil, thereby deepening its conflict with the Soviet Union. In return, Pakistan received considerable US economic and military aid which emboldened the military's grip over the Pakistani state and society, and the creation of a "garrison state".[10] The Nixon administration's sending of the 7th fleet led by the USS Enterprise into the Bay of Bengal during the Bangladesh War in 1971 showed the possibility of direct coercive action on the part of the United States. The US tilt was also prompted by the India–USSR quasi-alliance which emerged in the backdrop of the US–China–Pakistan entente. Balance of power politics was well alive in South Asia during the tumultuous years of the 1970s.

The Soviet invasion of Afghanistan in 1979 set in motion a powerful wave of superpower involvement in South Asia. The defeat and disorderly withdrawal of the Soviet forces in 1989 and the emergence of the Taliban in Afghanistan in 1996 brought considerable insecurity to the region. The Taliban also brought al-Qaeda to the region by sheltering Osama bin Laden and his network of terrorists. Pakistan played a crucial role in the rise of the Taliban and its deepening involvement with al-Qaeda and other terrorist groups in the region. Matters came to a sudden turn following the terrorist attacks in New York and Washington on September 11, 2001. The attackers were all connected to al-Qaeda and the US reacted with a military intervention and subsequent toppling of the Taliban regime, an action that Pakistan reluctantly agreed to support. American-led coalition efforts

---

[10] Lawrence Ziring, "Weak State, Failed State, Garrison State: The Pakistan Saga", in *South Asia's Weak States*, ed. T. V. Paul.

in Afghanistan to wipe out the Taliban have been ongoing since 2002. This involvement has seen only partial success as the Taliban operates from both sides of the Pakistan–Afghanistan border which the Pakistani army has not been able to fully control or is unwilling to do so.

The US military presence in the Afghanistan and Pakistan border areas has not resulted in increasing schism with India, at least during the George W. Bush years. There has been a warming of relations between the US and India and an improving of trade relations between India and China, despite their ongoing territorial dispute. There has been a decreasing interest of Russia in the sub-continent (except as a supplier of arms to India). However, China's activism in some South Asian and neighbouring states, especially in Pakistan and Myanmar and increasingly in Nepal, and India's efforts to counter it, have generated competitive dynamics in the sub-system's security environment. The un-demarcated India–China border has also witnessed several incursion incidents and acrimonious media reports in 2009. During the past few years, the competition between India and China for natural resources has also expanded to Africa, Central Asia and Latin America. In recent years, the United States has shown some equidistance between India and Pakistan and has encouraged the peace process between the two states (stalled due to the terrorist attacks in Mumbai in November 2008), but the military option is still its dominant approach to the war on the Taliban and al-Qaeda in Afghanistan and Pakistan. The Obama administration has shown less willingness to accommodate India in its efforts to acquire a major power status than the previous Bush administration did. The administration's efforts to befriend China and give Pakistan a prominent role in the Afghan war have led to considerable disquiet in India, although outwardly both India and the US are keeping their friendly approaches toward each other. The efforts by the US to cosy up to China may be linked to that country's enormous economic clout, especially through its holding of major US debt in the form of treasury bonds.

Despite the major power activism in the region, South Asia cannot be characterised as a hegemonic system (unlike Latin America and to an extent the Middle East) as the two dominant states of the region, India and Pakistan, carry considerable capacity to withstand such pressures. India, with over 70 percent of the population and economic strength of the region, especially is seeking an autonomous power position, i.e. great power status, in its own right based on its hard and soft power attributes. It attempted non-alignment as a strategy to maintain strategic autonomy from the two superpowers and the Cold War alignments which it was invited to join. It was partially successful in creating a sort of Third World activism, especially at the UN bodies, although when it came to intense conflicts with China and Pakistan it had to relax some of the principles of non-alignment. Today, India is seeking a major power role by engaging all leading states. India's claim is based on its rapidly accelerating economic growth (since 1991), expanding crucial military strength, especially in the nuclear and naval capabilities, and role in key global institutions. Its soft power assets also have been increasingly recognised as important in an era of globalisation.[11] In 2009, it has made some limited successes by first engaging the G-8 countries and by helping to get more clout for G-20 which includes several developing countries, and by convincing the Western countries to reassess voting rights at the IMF and World Bank. However, on some core issues like nuclear test ban, climate change, and Doha trade rounds, India seems at odds with Western positions, thereby creating some dissonance in their relationships. The simple fact that these are expressed and sorted out through global institutions offers much promise for India's peaceful rise in the international arena.

Future Patterns of Major Power Intervention in South Asia

Major powers are likely to stay active in South Asia for the foreseeable future. The two factors that I identified, geostrategic salience and the

---

[11] On these, see Baldev Raj Nayar and T.V. Paul, *India in the World Order: Searching for Major Power Status* (Cambridge: Cambridge University Press, 2002), pp. 48–63. See also Kishore Mahbubani, *The New Asian Hemisphere: The Irresistible Shift of Global Power to the East* (New York: Public Affairs, 2008).

presence of weak states, will bedevil South Asia for decades to come. The increasing power capabilities of China and India will also attract major powers such as the US and Russia to the region in their efforts to court or balance the rising powers. In particular, the growing economic prowess of China and India will attract major and minor power interests in these countries. However, it is the strategic context, i.e. the ongoing conflicts of the region, that is the most significant reason for continued major power activism in the region.

The Afghan conflict remains the most virulent asymmetric war in the early 21st century. The US, under the Obama administration, attaches great importance to this theatre. This would mean the US presence in Afghanistan and by extension Pakistan will continue until an amicable settlement is feasible, which is highly unlikely in the foreseeable future. Even if there is great domestic pressure on the US administration to withdraw from Afghanistan, the likelihood of the Taliban and al-Qaeda returning to power could force Washington to be active in the volatile region for some time to come. The key stumbling blocks for peace in Afghanistan are the absence of a national symbol to coalesce the various tribes and ethnic groups of Afghanistan, the absence of a democratic tradition and the temptation of the Taliban and radical Islamic groups to oppose whatever political system is installed there, other than theirs. The failed state of Afghanistan is the fundamental problem for the prospects of a peaceful regional order as the state is unlikely to exert control over the various parts of the country without massive propping up by external powers.[12] Furthermore, being in a central strategic location and a generator of regional and international disorder, Afghanistan is likely to receive great power attention more than its due share. Within the South and Central Asian region, it will also be a source of contention among the chief rivals — India and Pakistan — for influence peddling. Much attention is needed to manage the extraordinary interests of the regional powers in Afghanistan, and to transform Afghanistan into a normal state, a task that no major power is currently able to accomplish.

---

[12] On this, see Rasul Bakhsh Rais, "Afghanistan: A Weak State in the Path of Power Rivalries", in *South Asia's Weak States*, ed., T. V. Paul, Ch. 9.

Pakistan's engagements in Afghanistan have not been conducive to the stabilisation of the country. The Pakistani elite have a 19th century British-era understanding of the role of Afghanistan in Pakistan's security and power status. They appear to believe that Afghanistan should remain as their vassal, providing strategic depth to Pakistan itself. This would ensure also that Kabul will not abuse problems in the Pashtun regions of Pakistan and that it will not fall into the hands of Indian or Russian influence. Creating a strong, independent Afghanistan thus is viewed in Islamabad as not in Pakistan's vital interests. Many stakeholders in Islamabad will do everything in their power to undermine Afghanistan as an independent, strong nation-state. While the logic behind a weak Afghanistan is intuitively appealing to the Pakistani elite, it is based on a British-era geopolitical understanding of vassals and buffer states that violates the very principle of sovereign equality of states and non-intervention in each other's affairs. By seeking hegemony over Afghanistan, Pakistan is liable to the same criticism that it levels toward India of seeking hegemony in the region.

While India has done much to support Afghanistan's economic reconstruction, it is also keenly interested in the strategic and political fate of Afghanistan. Not only is India's security tied to that of Afghanistan's future, but so is its position in Central Asia with which it has had deep historical, cultural and economic links. Moreover, a Taliban-controlled Afghanistan would be a major source of jihadists fighting in Kashmir. It would also close India's opening to Central Asia as a key source of oil and natural gas. This means India will not abandon Afghanistan easily even if it scales down its reconstruction efforts, giving Pakistan a strong rationale to try to control Afghanistan. However, the Indian side may have to come up with more creative ways of dealing with Afghanistan as the lingering conflict there is bound to create high levels of insecurity for itself. Any settlement with Pakistan over Kashmir should also include removing Afghanistan as a persistent source of conflict between the two states. This means a joint recognition by New Delhi and Islamabad of the need to maintain Afghanistan's independent status, perhaps as a neutral power, taking into account the vital interests of the two neighboring states. Greater transparency and consultation may be needed to avoid many of the misconceptions that seem to bedevil their policies in Afghanistan.

Pakistan, despite bearing the brunt of externally driven interventions, is unlikely to abandon its links with major powers, the US and China. Bureaucratic and political actors within Pakistan are often tempted to pursue "double games" fearing that the end of conflicts in the region would affect their power position internally and the value the external powers attach to Pakistan as an ally. Pakistan's garrison state has survived for over 60 years despite its immense difficulties in nation-building because of the rents it receives through participation in great power conflicts.[13] This source of revenue is very tempting for the military to continue to receive and that means security business and conflict are often crucial to the economic and corporatist interests of the military. The absence of a powerful middle class and a civil society that can exert effective pressure for a proper democratic order in Pakistan is part of the reason for the military's dominance in that country.

The continued India–Pakistan rivalry will also attract great power interests in the region. Indeed it is the US that has acted as a mediator during intense crises in recent times involving these two nuclear-armed states. For instance, in the 1999 Kargil conflict, it was President Bill Clinton who intervened and convinced then Prime Minister Nawaz Sharif to withdraw Pakistani forces from the Kargil hills in an effort to prevent the escalation of the conflict.[14] The chance of future crises resulting from attacks by Pakistan-based terrorist groups in India cannot be ruled out. In that event, once again the US will be called upon to play the role of the mediator. It appears that the US role is positive in this regard, but the tendency on the part of Pakistan and India (to a limited extent) to engage in brinkmanship

---

[13] Stephen Philip Cohen, *The Idea of Pakistan* (Washington, DC: Brookings Institution Press, 2004), pp. 3–4; Husain Haqqani, *Pakistan: Between Mosque and Military* (Washington, DC: Carnegie Endowment for International Peace, 2005).

[14] On this, see Peter R. Lavoy, ed., *Asymmetric Warfare in South Asia: The Causes and Consequences of the Kargil Conflict* (Cambridge: Cambridge University Press, 2009).

policies with the understanding that the US would help prevent major escalation is a risky strategy indeed.

In terms of the balance of power politics, South Asia might witness increasing great power attention as the two rising powers China and India, by their very position in the emerging international system, will attract such attention. The changing dynamics in the relationships between India and China, India and Pakistan, Pakistan and China and Pakistan and the US are critical here. If China–India rivalry emerges as an intense conflict over the next few decades, it may have a major impact on the conflict patterns in the region. China is then likely to strengthen its relationship with Pakistan in an effort to fortify its balance of power position *vis-à-vis* India. India may try to counteract this with alignments with like-minded states of East and Southeast Asia. Furthermore, China's expanding interests in the Indian Ocean rim states impinge greatly on India's calculations of security. Both states are developing blue-water navies and are competing in Myanmar, Bangladesh, Nepal and Sri Lanka. China's naval activism somewhat challenges India's dominant status in the Indian Ocean region. For these and other reasons, the Sino–Indian rivalry has a real possibility to intensify as the century advances, a theme that I will return to subsequently.

Future US involvement in South Asia

Among the major powers, the US plays the dominant role in South Asia and its policies have the most consequence for the region's security order. During the Cold War, it was a key player with its off and on alignment with Pakistan, but also a power that played a significant role *vis-à-vis* India. With the end of the Cold War, the American role in the region underwent substantial changes. The Soviet withdrawal from Afghanistan also led to American withdrawal from Pakistan and Afghanistan, leaving the region to the vicissitudes of regional players, especially the Taliban. Washington is unlikely to abandon South Asia or the Indian Ocean in the foreseeable future due to the importance of Afghanistan and Pakistan and the Persian Gulf region with its developing conflict relationship with Iran. There are signs of

Washington playing a more constructive role in the region as well. In October 2009, the US Congress passed an Aid Bill which contained some provisions for Pakistan using it for domestic development and waging the war against the Taliban and not diverting the funds for its conflict with India.[15]

China's rising role in South Asia

China plays a crucial role in South Asia's conflict patterns. Its engagement has been one largely of the balance-of-power variety, although in recent years it has also been a major economic player in the region and a source of important infrastructure development. As Pakistan's key supplier of arms (including, in the past, nuclear materials and weapon designs) China is the most significant balancer against India. Despite their mutual antagonism, China has also developed an active trade relationship with India and today China has emerged as the leading trading partner of India. This is a paradox because rival states rarely trade with each other. China's ongoing territorial conflict with India, its long-lasting strategic relations with Pakistan, and its plans for active presence in the Indian Ocean and its littoral states all portend an emerging conflict relationship with India. The simple fact that, by around 2030, China will emerge as the leading economic power of the world, to be followed by the US and India, would mean the region becoming more crucial to the global economic order as well. China's "middle kingdom" attitude toward the regional order and the fact that only India in Asia can offer any substantial challenge to China would mean these two powers engaging in a rivalry relationship. At the same time, if the trend continues with respect to their increasing economic trade and interdependence, some level of mitigation in conflict is likely. Active territorial disputes add to the mix of rivalry between the two. Much attention is needed to prevent an

---

[15] Anwar Iqbal, "US Congress approves new restrictions on military aid", *The Dawn*, October 22, 2009 (http://www.dawn.com/wps/wcm/connect/dawn-content-library/dawn/news/world/12-us+congress+approves+new+restrictions+on+military+aid-bi-07).

inadvertent or deliberate war escalating from the propaganda campaign that each undertakes on a regular basis. Despite these trends, for the next decade or so, the region is unlikely to witness active balance of power politics involving military alliances and intense arms buildups. Much of the dynamics will be in the form of soft balancing and pre-balancing involving limited ententes, moderate levels of arms buildup and institutional bargaining.[16]

What Can Major Powers Do to Mitigate Conflict in South Asia?

Major powers can offer a lot of constructive policies in reducing conflict in South Asia. They can prod the regional states to move away from hard realpolitik competition that they often engage into an order based on the principles of the Kantian tripod — democratic governance, regional institutions and economic interdependence — and thereby help to create a limited peaceful security community. These Kantian principles could form key components of regional security based on the notion of cooperative security as opposed to competitive outbidding. This would mean resisting the temptation to provide arms and ammunition to regional states without substantial pre-conditions, and intervention in territorial and ethnic conflicts within the regional states. Major powers can help to develop deeper institutional links and economic interdependencies among the regional states as they are doing in Southeast Asia.

The role of regional states

It is a myth that the regional states do not play any big role in bringing great powers to a region. In South Asia, the regional states have quite a bit of leeway in determining how much great power intervention is tolerated. If they want to avoid such involvement, they have to be careful not to engage in too much external balancing using

---

[16] For these strategies, see T. V. Paul, "Soft Balancing in the Age of US Primacy", *International Security*, 30 (Summer 2005) 46–71.

great power allies. When smaller South Asian states excessively engage in balancing strategies, they can attract India's wrath as it will feel considerably threatened by such actions. Given the asymmetry in size and their dependence on India, such a strategy is unlikely to succeed. However, it is also important that India creates reasonable conditions for the minor states to tackle their security and developmental problems in a cooperative fashion.

A major challenge for South Asian states is to abandon their interventionist tendencies in each other's affairs. This means that if it wants to obtain peace in South Asia, Pakistan has to abandon its intervention often carried out through terrorist outfits in India, especially in Kashmir. Similarly, India should refrain from intervening in Pakistan's Baluchistan province, Pakistan in Afghanistan and Afghanistan in Pakistan by way of support for Pashtun nationalism. These states may have to accept territorial status quo or territorial compromises based on peaceful methods rather than asymmetric violent methods. Territorial revisionism is fraught with dangers as more and more ethnic groups will want to separate if they sense the central governments are willing to concede. In comparison with Southeast Asia, Latin America and to a certain extent Africa, South Asian states wilfully or otherwise intervene in each other's affairs, despite holding very strong notions of sovereignty. This continuous violation of the territorial integrity norm has created much ill will and suspicion in the region.

The regional states can also create regional institutions similar to the ASEAN Regional Forum (ARF) in Southeast Asia to engage major powers and key regional states. These talking shops can do a lot of service in limiting regional and major power conflicts by allowing them a regular forum to discuss regional and global issues. The "ASEAN way", for instance, comprises less of a proactive regional security provider than a socio-cultural complex of sovereignty, the non-use of force and the peaceful settlement of disputes, founded on "informality", "consultations" and "consensus", rather than a supranational security architecture.[17] This means the South Asian

---

[17] Amitav Acharya, *Constructing a Security Community in Southeast Asia: ASEAN and the Problem of Regional Order* (London: Routledge, 2001), p. 26.

Association for Regional Cooperation (SAARC) has to become a lot more effective as an institution for diplomacy and confidence building not only among the regional states, but between the regional states and major powers.

Conclusion

This chapter sketched out the two critical dimensions for great power involvement in South Asia, the region's geostrategic salience and the presence of several weak states with intense conflict dynamics among them. It also showed how these twin elements worked during the Cold War era and how it is changing in the post-Cold War era. The role of the region in the 9/11 attacks and the following events in Afghanistan have shown the increasing interest of the US in the region. Today, great power interest in the region is assuming a new dimension with the increasing economic and military strength of China and India and their potential for an accelerated rivalry in the Asia–Pacific region as they emerge as key global powers. Although their balancing behavior currently is muted and largely relies on soft balancing and pre-balancing, an intense balance-of-power competition is possible if US–China and China–India relations deteriorate and the great power system witnesses a power transition conflict in the future. Much deeper strategic engagement and institution-based cooperation are needed to avoid the occurrence of such conflicts in the region.

Chapter 6

Religious Extremism and Terrorism in Pakistan: Challenges for National Security

Rasul Bakhsh Rais

Religion is one of the old sources of social cohesion as well as conflict. While common faith, values and religious practices create a sense of community among the believers of the same creed or sect, it also distinguishes them from other similar communities founded on a different faith. Modernity, the nation-state and ideas of secularism in most of the countries around the world have created larger political communities accepting religious, cultural and ethnic pluralism. The modern nation-state provides a constitutional and legal framework for equal citizenship giving individuals freedom to adopt any belief system and practise it. Therefore, what binds the political communities and gives them a sense of togetherness is not religion but a nation and the state as its political expression. The question of neutrality of the state in religious matters is somewhat settled in Western societies. This is not the case in Pakistan or some other Muslim societies where we find Islamist groups trying to redefine the relationship of religion with the state and political authority. In this chapter, we raise two questions: How do religious discourses and identity politics associated with them contribute to sectarian intolerance and violence? How is weakness of the state or "ineffective statehood" responsible for religious violence? In answering these questions, the essay premises on the following two hypotheses:

1. In societies like Pakistan where religion dominates the social and political discourses and defines a sense of large community,

a balance between religious and political sphere has yet to be negotiated.

2. Authoritarian regimes in Pakistan, by clogging channels of interest articulation and participation, have magnified the power and influence of religious groups and their quest to determine the relationship of religion with the state.

Religion, State and Society

The question of where religion should be situated in the state and society in this modern age raises troublesome controversies in the Muslim countries. During the age of empires, however, this issue had largely been settled.

Muslim empires worked on the principle of two spheres, one of religion and the other of the secular Muslim rulers. The two spheres operated mostly independent of each other and understood well their limits and jurisdictional boundaries. Each accorded respect to the other. The Muslim jurists placed only two limitations on the Muslim ruler: he should be just, and he must not enact rules against the well-recognised streams of Islamic law. This principle allowed the Muslim societies to achieve a great degree of balance and the equation between the spiritual and temporal worlds worked to the benefit of both. The secular ruler got the allegiance (political legitimacy) while the ulema and their religious networks enjoyed the autonomy and freedom to educate the masses and spread the world of God without any hindrance from the emperor.

Western imperialism heralded the arrival of the modern age. Social responses to Western domination were shaped largely by the ideology of nationalism and later defined by alternative approaches to the reconstruction of a national state and a search for its ideological identity. In the Muslim-dominated communities, it was more than decolonisation; it was also a quest for rediscovery of the lost self under foreign rule, primarily of culture, classical knowledge and political power. The social and political activities of the Muslim communities associated with recovery of the past and shaping of future visions and plans brought the religion back to the centre of their political discourse.

Therefore, the rise of political Islam is not entirely a new phenomenon, as is generally misunderstood. It began with an internal intellectual inquiry in the religious circles of the Muslim societies in the subcontinent and the Middle East when independence appeared over the horizon. This was also a time when competing ideologies, old and new, began to demonstrate greater influence than anytime before or during the last century. For the Muslims, it was a defining moment in terms of choosing an ideological direction with powerful pulls of socialism, democracy and capitalism. Undoubtedly, these three streams of ideology were part of the modern world and along with secular ideas that had impacted certain sections of the Muslim societies.

The Islamic thinkers, scholars and activists that founded the Ikhwan ul Muslimoon in the Middle East and Jama'at-e Islami in India, as did others in their individual capacity, began to conceive of Islam as an alternative ideology to order social, economic and political life in the postcolonial state.[1] They were impressed by the appeal of ideology in their times and, more importantly, by the organisational style, methods of recruitment, indoctrination and discipline of Fascist and Communist parties of Europe. The Ikhwan and the Jama'at and other religious parties in the Muslim world have followed similar patterns of recruiting, training and grooming their cadres for political activism and leadership roles. The central theme of all religio-political parties has been and is likely to be in the coming decades that Muslim societies corrupted by colonial rule, Western influences and now increasingly by the onslaught of cultural globalisation need to be Islamised through the agency of the state.

This is where they would like to situate the religion, right at the centre, as the soul of Muslim society and the state. This is also what defines political Islam in our times. The quest and the struggle of the Islamists is centred around the notion that they must first capture the state and then use its expansive, coercive power to implement the Islamic law, promote virtue and stamp out vice. Mass

---

[1] Seyyed Vali Reza Nasr, *The Vanguard of Islamic Revolution: Jama'at-i-Islami of Pakistan* (Berkeley: University of California Press, 1994).

mobilisation, political pressure and threat of agitation are secondary options of the Islamists that they generally exercise from the outside of formal political structures for the implementation of the Islamic law when they are not in power. Over time, the religious parties have acquired critical political mass through various strategies of public welfare and grassroots organisational work, reaching out to professional groups and building coalitions with right-of-centre parties.[2]

Acquiring or accessing political power is a very important goal of all political parties, and religious parties are no exception in this respect. The only difference is that they justify their quest for power with reference to Islam, Islamisation programmes, and with an objective of creating an Islamic society in their image of religious purity, virtue and righteousness. They make a similar appeal to the society to return to the original ideals of Islam, as would any ideological political party trying to change the mindset. In this struggle and appeal, the religious parties have done well in presenting a coherent and persistent, although a simplistic critique of many failures of the postcolonial state governed by the corrupt elites. They present Islam and themselves as better alternatives to the ills of the modern nation-state. In doing so, they have carved up a good constituency of support among the lower middle classes and increasing disaffected and poor sections of both the rural as well as urban communities.

While other competing political groups in relatively more open Muslim polities like that of Pakistan recognise the right of religious parties to compete for power freely, they want them to stay within the limits of law and constitution. But the central political objective of the religious parties is not just acquiring power; they want a structural change in redefining the relationship of Islam with the state. This is however a minority view. At least in Pakistan, as for now, the question of placing religion in the domain of the state has not invoked unanimous political response. The reasons for the lack of any agreement on this issue among the Muslim communities and states all over the world are too obvious. Colonisation changed the very basis of

---

[2] Olivier Roy, *The Failure of Political Islam* (Cambridge: Harvard University Press, 1994).

authority and institutional order of the state from the minimal, indirect and less intrusive one of the medieval Muslim empires to a very expansive and coercive state. The modernity syndrome created by the Western imperial rule is in all important areas of societal life, from new educational systems to philosophy of life, class structure and the new modes of political economy.

It is this legacy of imperial inheritance that is at the root of many ideological controversies and political conflicts and power contests in most of the Muslim countries. It is more so in Pakistan because most of the religious parties and factions contest the meaning of the creation of Pakistan, which they believe was about creating an Islamic state.

It is clear that the Islamists contest for political power and once having it want to reshape state–society relations, pursuing Islamisation as the primary goal. In this quest, they want to restructure the postcolonial state and re-determine its path. The mainstream political parties and groups that have traditionally dominated the political arena have not rejected religion altogether in their political discourse and have used religion in critical political situations to compete with the religious parties. Their political use of religion has produced rather counter effects in blurred political boundaries between Islam and politics.

What role religion must play in the affairs of the state remains a contested issue with competing claims between religious parties and semi-secular to secular mainstream parties. It has not sunken deep into popular politics that religion is essentially a very private matter between man and his creator. To employ an external agency to promote spiritual and religious matters, especially when the agency is a modern state with the most coercive elements at its disposal, could turn it into an oppressive and totalitarian entity. Imbued with the spirit of authenticity, certitude and a mission, the religion-based political authority would turn intolerant. There is ample evidence of this from the experience of religious and ideological states of medieval and modern times. Repeating the same mistakes would really do Pakistan or any other society no good at all, further weaken religious unity, and sap collective energies.

Political Islam, which declares the separation of state and religion as heretical, is flawed in its attempt to employ the device of the state to enforce religious values. Religion belongs to the individual and to the community and is primarily a voluntary act. It is impossible for any law enforced by the state agencies to make individuals pious, righteous or even good human beings. The religious political parties think very differently on the relationship between Islam and the Pakistani state.

Sociology of Religious Resurgence

The religious political parties have been part of the social and political landscape of Pakistan and existed in some form even before the creation of the country in 1947.[3] In recent decades, their networks have expanded greatly. Three factors have contributed to their expansion. These are: the legacy of the Afghan war, spillover effects of the Iranian revolution and the generous flow of funds from the Gulf and the Middle East, both from private individuals and some governments. If not all, some of the madrasas have become political nurseries of the religious political parties. A good number of students and teachers from these institutions got recruited in the war of resistance against the former Soviet Union in Afghanistan and later became part of the Taliban fighting force.[4] This phenomenon has raised questions about the future role of the religious political parties in Pakistan and their political activism and how their discourse on political Islam feeds into sectarian divide, communal mindset and religious extremism.

Let us make it clear that the religious political parties do not share the political vision of the mainstream political parties or the founders of Pakistan on the identity of the country as a moderate Islamic state.

---

[3] Ishtiaq Hussain Qureshi, *Ulema in Politics: A Study Relating to the Political Activities of the Ulema in the South Asian Subcontinent from 1556 to 1947* (Karachi: Maaref, 1972).

[4] David B. Edwards, *Before the Taliban: Genealogies of the Afghan Jihad* (Berkeley: University of California Press, 2002).

They interpret the creation of the country as a quest for establishing an Islamic state. For the past 60 years, they have struggled to get Pakistan declared as an Islamic state, which is already an Islamic Republic at least by its official denomination. They want to establish *Sharia* or Islamic law as the supreme law of the land, enforce Islamic jurisprudence and change the political culture and institutions of the country according to their own understanding of Islam.[5] Their politics as well as interpretation of the rationale for the creation of Pakistan have been contested both by the bureaucratic-military elites and the mainstream political parties. What is their strength and how strong is their power base? Do they present any threat to the present government? In this section we will address these questions.

We need to understand the complex social, economic and political conditions that are contributing to the growth and, in certain sections of the society, popularity of the religious organisations in Pakistan. Among many reasons that might explain the growth of religious parties, military authoritarianism and the failure of the postcolonial state in satisfying popular expectations are two major causes. In our view these movements are a response to the inability of the governments to provide economic opportunities, political freedom, clean governance and an effective system of justice. A pertinent question is why hundreds of thousands of young students have gone to the madrasa networks that produce fixed, narrow and anti-modern mindsets? The answer is that the Pakistani state has failed to bring them into the modern educational institutions.[6]

Many governments in Pakistan have relied on coercive means to control dissent and political opposition, thus aggravating their legitimacy crisis. By suppressing the growth of even the most moderate of secular, democratic groups, they have unintentionally encouraged the spread of Islamic political influences. Consequently, by appropriating the nationalist, anti-imperialist agenda, the Islamist groups present

---

[5] Syed Abul Ala Maudoodi, *Islami Riasat* (Islamic State) (Lahore: Islamic Publications, 1967).

[6] "Pakistan: Madrasas, Extremism and the Military", Asia Report No. 36 (Brussels: International Crisis Group, July 29, 2002).

themselves as the only political alternative to the widely unpopular, pro-Western authoritarian regimes.

Like many Islamic countries, the state in Pakistan has been controlled by corrupt political elites who have failed to address the real issues of social development and distributive justice.[7] The masses are still caught in the web of illiteracy, soul-crushing poverty and backwardness, while the upper layers of society enjoy the most modern lifestyle and the benefits of economic growth. The Islamists' critique of the Pakistani state focuses on its structural as well as public policy problems. They argue that structurally the country has been deliberately removed from its religious moorings, cultural heritage and civilisational roots. The colonial pattern of government — such as in law, the judicial system, education, economy and political institutions — has not only been retained but also strengthened. They question the relevance of Western institutions and practices to the real needs of Pakistani society. This leads one to the complex debate on the issue of modernisation.

The Islamists insist that they are not against the development and modernisation of the economy, but their concern is how to hedge modernisation from political and cultural influences of the West. The fears of Western cultural domination are real, and the Islamists in Pakistan or elsewhere are as concerned as any other nationalist movement in a non-Islamic society.[8]

A second set of criticisms is directed at the role of the Pakistani elites, both civil and military, who have dominated the state apparatus. The political elites largely come from the land-owning class who, with rare exception, lack the understanding and knowledge of running a modern state. Even those who came from business and industrial backgrounds have a strong imprint of feudal culture on their political attitudes. With few exceptions, all of them have amassed private fortunes at public expense.

---

[7] M. Asghar Khan, *We Have Learnt Nothing from History: Pakistan, Politics and Military Power* (Karachi: Oxford University Press, 2005).

[8] Benjamin Barber, *Jihad Versus McWorld* (New York: Times Books, 1995).

What makes the issues of corruption and bad governance so important is that the common man has lost faith in the ability and sincerity of the present class of political leaders to provide an honest and clean government. By attacking the credibility of the political leaders and their parties, the religious groups present themselves and their vision of the Islamic system as an alternative to the existing one. Frustrated by the traditional elites, some actors of the Pakistani society, particularly the lower middle classes, look towards the religious parties as a better political alternative.

How likely are the Islamists to win the hearts and minds of the people of Pakistan? Although they remain very important political players and some of them are more organised than secular political parties, they do not seem to pose a challenge to the power and position of the traditional elites and mainstream political parties. This is demonstrated by their dismal performance in successive general elections in Pakistan. The election in 2002 was a departure from the past pattern as far as the electoral performance of the religious parties is concerned. It was for two reasons. First, the religious parties formed an alliance that saved them from dividing their votes. The second factor that contributed to their victory was the American war in Afghanistan, which they used very effectively to put forward an anti-American plank.[9] The religious groups do not have a broad support base in the society. All religious groups have factions and are divided along political, sectarian and narrow doctrinal lines. And rarely have they demonstrated unity on any single national issue.

The feudal base of politics in the country has kept the religious leaders on the margins of social influence. Therefore, in vast rural communities, the religious parties lack the following and have, so far, failed to make inroads into the traditional constituency of the land-owning class. They may capitalise on the growing alienation of the lower middle classes in the urban areas, use effectively the street power that they have and forge close alliances among themselves in future. Our contention in this chapter is that political Islam, even

---

[9] Mohammad Waseem, *Demoratisation in Pakistan: A Study of 2002 Elections* (Karachi: Oxford University Press, 2006).

staying within the limits of constitutionality, has indirectly contributed to the formation of sectarian identities and to violence associated with it.

Religious Extremism

What threatens Pakistan's security today is religious extremism. It is sadly true that religious and sectarian extremism has been on the rise in Pakistan for the past three decades. There has been some ebb and flow, but no sign of resolution of the problem. We have witnessed terrible acts of collective violence, assaults on religious congregations, bombings of mosques and revenge killings between Sunni fanatics and Shiite militants. This conflict has grown horizontally and vertically, hurting more families in different areas of the country.[10] With religious extremism and intolerance on the rise, communal identities have become stronger and more visible than they were about a quarter of a century back.

People belonging to different sects have adopted distinctive attires, styles of mosque architecture and unique religious observances and celebrations. Gone are the days when members of different sectarian communities used to pray and observe religious festivals together. Feelings of otherness and alienation have grown deeper and the arrival of the suicide bomber has made anyone entering the mosque of another sect suspect.

What has really contributed to religious extremism and sectarianism? The answer to this involves political, religious and social categories.[11] Politics is the master science of society. Therefore, if anything goes woefully wrong, as it clearly does in religious violence, we must look at the character of regimes, their legitimacy, political ends and manner of exercising power. We have already alluded to some of these factors.

---

[10] Mukhtar Ahmad Ali, "Sectarian Conflict in Pakistan", Policy Studies 9 (Colombo: Regional Centre for Strategic Studies, 2000), p. 14.

[11] See some of the explanation in Mohammad Waseem, "Sectarian Conflict in Pakistan", in K.M. de Silva (ed.), *Conflict and Violence in South Asia* (Kandi, Sri Lanka: International Centre for Ethnic Studies, 2000), pp. 20–21.

The last military regime with a democratic civilian façade was greatly responsible for the rise of religious extremism. Despite the official vocabulary of "enlightened moderation" and the government's habit of blaming its present troubles on past rulers, its suppression and fragmentation of the mainstream political parties created greater larger political and social space for the religious groups.[12]

The religious set of reasons that we can ascribe to extremism are often ignored in the political and social discourse in Pakistan. Theological and doctrinal differences are normal in religious communities, but keeping peace between them requires tolerance in a pluralistic framework. Pakistani society and the traditional clergymen representing different sects lived in harmony and accepted the legitimacy of having differences and the rights of the individual to select a faith or sect and practise it in his or her own way. All that has gradually changed; conformity has replaced the traditional values of respect and tolerance for the beliefs of others.

Neither intellectual nor official outfits have paid great attention to the sectarian mullah and the poison that he frequently spouts from his unholy pulpit. Some mullahs with brand names and notoriety specialise in demonising other faiths and sects. Cassettes, loudspeakers and printed sectarian material are still in use, but in recent decades they have added new technological weapons to their arsenal of hate: websites, computer disks and mass e-mailing.[13]

Freedom of speech is a fundamental right of every citizen, but must correspond with the obligation to respect other's rights. Hate speech and materials, delivered from the platform of the mosque, theoretically a neutral, spiritual place open to worship for all Muslims, and from homes and workplaces must not be tolerated. They engender violence and create rifts in the society. Law, if there is any, and its execution has been ineffective in dealing with the sectarian mullah.

---

[12] I.A. Rehman, "Politics of Religion", *Newsline*, October, 1999.

[13] Interrogation of sectarian terrorists reveals that they resorted to violent acts against the religious leaders of other sects on account of hate literature. See Shaukat Javed, PSP, *Sectarian Terrorism in Pakistan: Challenges and Response* (Islamabad: National Defence College, National Defence Course, 2001–2002), pp. 12–19.

Lastly, social reasons are no less important in encouraging religious extremism and sectarianism than the failure of government. The state is primarily responsible for maintaining law and order, protecting the citizens and bringing sectarian criminals to justice, but that does not absolve the society altogether. Socially aware and active societies have soft power that they can use to ostracise, marginalise and openly condemn religious violence, hate and communalism. By growing religious in a wrong way, Pakistani society has not publicly denounced religious violence in a politically significant way. Silence on sectarian-motivated violence and murders and now the passive approval of Talibanisation in the tribal belt provide us with enough clues about how a non-activist, parochial and communalised society encourages extremism.

Sectarian madrasas and mullahs challenging the writ of the state both in the rural, tribal periphery and the urban areas have been supported by the society. The urban middle class, with a conservative and sectarian mindset, meets most of their material needs in return for expected spiritual rewards. This is an atrocious manifestation of religiosity.

The danger is that allegiance to sect and faith may replace Pakistani citizens' fundamental commitment and obligation to state and nationhood. The mullahs, whose feelings for the Pakistani state as envisioned by its founders are extremely weak, continue to challenge this vision by insisting on transforming the country into a theocratic state. If not the religious political parties, other groups like the Taliban would not hesitate to use force to establish an Islamic order in their narrow vision in pockets of the country, as they have been trying to do in some of the tribal areas.

In our view, violence is both a political statement as well as an instrument of political empowerment. Conduct of violence, ethnic as well as religious, whether you call it sectarian terrorism or by any other name, is instrumental; it has a political purpose and those engaged in it have a well-defined strategy behind it. We need to understand why they have taken the deadly path to power. The answer is simple but very bitter: because the normal democratic route has been clogged for too long, normal expression of politics through democratic means has quite often been disrupted, and those who claim representation in the mainstream political parties have false mandate. It is absolutely false because the contest or representation is confined to powerful clans, families, tribes and castes. Other political aspirants stay either on the margins or join them as courtiers, flatterers and sycophants.

The denial of true democracy and absence of institutionalised politics have turned both the new middle classes as well as the marginalised sections toward ethnic and religious parties. The other important reason is the failure of the Pakistani state in providing good governance, running a good economy or in delivering vital services. Resource crunch is the usual argument for this failure. I think it is, but it is not the sole reason; there is also massive corruption in the government departments, from top to bottom, scandalous looting of national wealth by some members of the elite club, and rapid decline in the governing capacity of the state institutions. One of the side effects of the corruption of Pakistani elites is a substantial increase in poverty, both rural as well as urban. Because corruption does not allow the state to perform its extractive function and redistribute the national wealth for the social welfare of the poor or society in general. Many of the benefits of economic progress have remained within the elite network. Will not this state of affairs drive the poor, new middle classes toward desperation? It has indeed, and Pakistan is reaping partly the effects of our bad politics in the rise of violence.

There are some structural reasons that we need to consider as well. Many bouts of power struggles within the elite club have left the state institutions weak and ineffective. There is a general consensus within the country on the Pakistani state being weak, ineffective and soft. Unless the Pakistani leaders recognise what has gone really wrong, they cannot address the problem of political violence by administrative measures alone. They have applied these measures quite often, which have not worked, and I am afraid they may not work in future. They must start working with the basics, which are: allowing democratic politics to grow, but not that which is confined to the elite club; increasing the administrative and political capacity of the state; conducting accountability of the members of the elite

club; making the judiciary a strong, independent and powerful institution; recognising the professional autonomy of all government
departments, more significantly than that of the police, so that these
are not used by the elite club as an instrument of protecting and promoting self-interests. Pakistan needs to create a new politics that truly
represents the new classes and reflects the change in Pakistani society
before the new middle classes start exploring the Islamist options.

The Question of Tolerance

In recent decades, the social trends in Pakistani society have changed
a bit for the worse. It is no longer accommodative of or tolerant
toward religious differences as it used to be. The trend is toward
promoting dominant majority views on religion and religious values.
There are many causes for this, but among the salient ones is the failure to develop educational institutions into places of free debate and
inquiry. We cannot expect it to happen with the poor quality of
academic leadership and political expediency guiding the policies of
governments.

I am focusing more on modern institutions than on other factors
in this section for an obvious reason: the primary function and the
historical identity of the academy is associated with the training of
free-thinking, rational, tolerant and open individuals who develop
themselves to respecting others and giving equal value to beliefs other
than their own. I think a good number of graduates and the majority
of those who are imparting modern knowledge in Pakistan lack these
essential qualities of a modern person.

Let me also discuss briefly two other reasons for the growth
of extremism and violence. The first is the poor delivery of social
services. Contrary to official claims, the Pakistani system of governance has been in constant decline for decades. Even if we take the
first principle, law and order, the primary responsibility of the government, we see a poor record of the Islamic Republic. Most of the
questions about law and order become centred on the fundamental
rights of the individual — life, property and, in the Lockean sense,
pursuit of liberty. Property rights are poorly enforced; life, if not

short and brutish, its fullness and self-actualisation is uncertain and problematic; and liberty is hostage to tradition, conservative religious values and a hybrid of feudal-military authoritarianism. The combination of these forces over time has created an intolerant society because all elements of the iron triangle — mullah, military and the feudals — by their class interests and organisational culture seek conformity and punish dissent.

I believe we need to look at the socialisation and culture of Pakistan's ruling elites in order to understand why the state and society view violence against women and religious minorities with a great deal of permissiveness. Our debate about the failure of the state in dealing with religious, ethnic and sectarian violence often revolves around its capacities. That is true, but not enough of an explanation. The general mindset of the three major groups that I have referred to above and their attitudes, values and orientation toward accommodation of difference need to be looked at closely to understand the ineffectiveness of the government.

But above all it is the growing numbers of men and women who think it is their primary religious duty to make other Muslims believe and behave like them. They are possessed with an artificial sense of certitude, authenticity and being on the right path to influence others' religious and social choices. A good number of them have become self-appointed soldiers of God, His judges and executioners, practising violence in stateless spaces in the borderlands. Violence motivated by religious considerations is not so infrequent and takes the many forms of humiliation, physical assault and target killings of prominent religious scholars, professionals and community leaders of rival sects and those violating the religious code.

I believe religion has a great value in answering questions about the mystery of existence and giving a positive and purposive direction to a person's life. But we cannot rely on religion alone to create a peaceful, orderly and tolerant society. An individual made up of greed, ambition and lust for power cannot be tamed by religious values alone. This role has to be played by the state through its strong arm of law. But then, law cannot be strong enough without the rule of law. Here, we are back to the basics.

Never will intolerance and violence disappear from Pakistani or any society for that matter with the sermons, speeches and florid statements of religious and political leaders. In the case of Pakistan, what is required is a process of structural reforms starting with the governance and educational system. This must be done urgently. Effecting social change and modern rational attitudes of tolerance of difference is a long-term process, but Pakistan must set itself on this long journey by investing more in social development and by making calculated interventions through law and public policy into the structures of the rural areas.

The Taliban and Violence

We are not sure if the Pakistani Taliban and their brand of justice and political violence ever had grassroots public support. There is only one objective measurement of public support, and that is the percentage of the popular votes a party or group wins at the elections. The Taliban and their public defenders, with their numbers on a constant decline, do not have trust in the common man nor seek power through popular legitimacy. Their route to power is through tribal-type conquest and absolute subjugation of the people to their interpretation of religion.

But then the Taliban are a very different kind of people: they do not accept democracy, the constitution, fundamental human rights, equality among citizens or the sovereignty of parliament. Nor do they represent Islam as it is understood and interpreted by great classical or modern-day Muslim scholars and jurists.

The Taliban, those who have taken up arms against the people, society and state of Pakistan, have neither learnt the ethical, philosophical and cultural content of Islam nor have they any respect for religious pluralism within the broader understanding of Islam as it is practised by different streams of religious thought in different countries.

How did they emerge as a religious and militant force?

The political and ideological roots of the Pakistani Taliban are in the Taliban movement of Afghanistan and its successful overthrow of the fragmented Mujahideen government in 1996. Two other factors need to be mentioned regarding their rise. First is the Pashtun ethnicity and the philosophy of tribal warfare to redress wrong, seek justice, punish wrongdoers, and establish their control and political domination.

The second is Pakistan's covert alliance with the Taliban as a formidable demographic and military force against other ethnic groups in Afghanistan, which were supported by the rival regional powers — Iran, India and Russia. Many political leaders in Pakistan and in other countries thought the Taliban were a good force as long as they could end violence and warlordism, establish peace and security and de-weaponise Afghan society.

Since the Mujahideen war against the Soviet Union, private Pakistani religious groups along with the Pakistani government and Western powers became deeply involved in Afghanistan. It was a strange mix of powers with different post-Soviet outlooks for the region. They were rooted in different ideological and cultural traditions but they had an immediate common goal: defeat of the Soviet Union and the Afghan communists.

The Pakistani Taliban tradition — armed struggle by mainly religious groups to establish an Islamic regime — is based on history, factional beliefs and political ethos linked to the Afghan Taliban. In terms of ideology, political purpose and even operational strategy, the Pakistani and Afghan Taliban, despite denials, are not two very different entities.

The closet Taliban in the Pakistani media, the religious and political parties, and some political commentators created a benign myth about the Taliban as an Islamic force willing to sacrifice anything to defeat Western imperialism and its surrogate elites in Afghanistan and Pakistan. A wide array of other Muslim groups from the Middle East have similar agendas and have transnational linkages through Al-Qaeda and other organisations to fund and promote this mindset.

The Taliban mindset further flourished during the Musharraf regime as it encouraged, courted and supported the religious parties. These parties after the widely rigged elections of 2002 formed governments in two critical provinces — Balochistan and the NWFP, both bordering Afghanistan, where a Taliban insurgency was underway. It was really during the tenure of General Musharraf that the Pakistani Taliban became more organised in Swat, Malakand, and the FATA, taking control of territory through the use of violence. Their occupation has been vacated but at huge human and material cost through a series of military operations in 2009–2010.

The anti-American sentiment in the context of Afghanistan was carefully cultivated by Taliban sympathisers in Pakistan, which further nurtured the image of the Taliban as an "anti-imperialist force" and some kind of liberator. Some leaders, mostly from the religious parties, justified crossing of the Pak–Afghan border by the Pakistani Taliban much like the Mujahideen that fought against the former Soviet Union.

The supporters of the Taliban, now silenced by the majority view, still do not see them as a threat to society and the state. It does not really matter to these Taliban supporters if people are humiliated, whipped or slaughtered publicly and on camera.

But finally, the people of Pakistan, the silent majority, have woken up to the threat that the Taliban and their supporters in different political formations pose to society and, in a broader context, to the image of Muslims and Islamic civilisation. The Taliban actually further the same caricatured view of Islam and Muslim societies as intolerant, primitive and hostile to modernity and human liberty as the one held by some Orientalists.

Pakistan's standing as an Islamic society suffered a great deal during the Musharraf regime as it was caught between the Taliban and him who had no respect for the constitution, the people's mandate or democratic principles.

As the fake democracy and political manipulations of the Musharraf regime and his political associates and their corruption have become exposed, so has the brutality and violent face of the Taliban. As the Taliban ordered suicide bombing of civilians, killed security personnel, targeted locally influential tribal elders and engaged in criminal activities to sustain their war against the Pakistani state and society, the people of Pakistan realised who the real enemy was.

The people in Swat and FATA were held hostage and suffered the cruelty and totalitarianism of the Taliban for too long. Neither the successive Pakistani governments nor the rest of society came to their rescue, while the Taliban's supporters continued to praise them as patriotic, just and selfless warriors.

A big shift in the image of the Taliban and their supporters has occurred, not accidentally but after a careful analysis of what Pakistan and its society would become if the Taliban and other religious zealots were allowed to capture power. Life in Pakistan under the Taliban or forces like them would fare no better than the Hobbesian state of nature — brutish, nasty and short.

The strong sentiment against the Taliban that has emerged is comparable to the patriotic sentiment during Pakistan's three wars with India. Many people in Pakistan and outside the country believe that the Taliban are a worse enemy than any other internal or external adversary that the country has ever faced.

This realisation, though late in the day, will help the security forces and the democratic government marginalise and effectively counter the Taliban threat. Pakistan has already secured a big victory against the Taliban by creating a national consensus against them. The Taliban and their supporters who scared the society for so long have suffered a big blow and may not be able to recover socially and politically. But this also offers Pakistan a respite and opportunity to address the domestic and foreign policy issues that created the Taliban monster in the first place.

The violent confrontation in Swat and now in South Waziristan has already produced some convulsive consequences in the regions bordering Afghanistan and in the settled areas of the Frontier Province and beyond into Islamabad and Lahore. The latest reactions of the militants give one the impression that caution and good sense are the last things on their mind.[14] It is time to ponder seriously the national security threat Pakistan might face from within in the coming months and perhaps years.

On one level, the threat is not entirely from within but in an ideological and strategic sense linked to a transnational militant Islam

---

[14] "Bloodbath in Peshawar: At Least 105 Killed, 200 Injured in Meena Bazaar Car Bombing", *Daily Times*, October 29, 2009.

with roots in Afghanistan and the Middle East. For decades, Pakistan played gracious host to militants and to absurdly grandiose strategic schemes, without reflecting for a moment on the adverse effects they had on state and society. Now is the time for truth, introspection and rational analysis: what harm has Pakistan done to itself and how can it redefine its future direction?

Pakistani governments have done enough scapegoating and blame-shifting. The ruling groups have no more time or political capital to waste on this; they must come to grips with the evolving challenge to the national solidarity and internal peace. And there is no bigger challenge to Pakistan's security today than the social gulf between the worldviews of mainstream society and the Taliban fringe.

Transfixed by the happenings in the tribal regions, the public might have noted how far apart madrasa-educated students and the clergy and the rest of society have drifted during the past three decades. They seem to have different ideals, feelings, worldviews and understanding of what is good for Muslims and Pakistan.

The madrasa network, fast expanding by taking over public spaces in and around towns, is not isolated. By offering care and education to the poor and marginalised sections of the most backward areas of the country, the madrasa has emerged as a relatively credible religious institution.[15] This is especially so in the estimation of the conservative, religiously orientated, urban middle class, which throws lot of money into it.

Judging from the way the vast majority of people in the street interpret political world and Islam and the West issues, it seems that extremism is no longer confined to what we have tended to regard as "fringe elements". An irrational, anti-modern and obscurantist mind-set, with a conspiratorial twist on everything that might matter in politics, is too apparent in everyday conversation even among university graduates, mature professionals and government functionaries.

---

[15] The number of madrasas (religious seminaries) is estimated to be around 17,000. The security agencies believe that out of this big number about 20 madrasas are involved in militancy in the country. See "Intelligence Agencies to Identify Troublesome Madrasas", *Daily Times*, July 20, 2007.

We in Pakistan have just begun to taste what extremism and violence can mean when terrorists win some social approval and religious authenticity. Muslims in the larger Middle East region have responded to humiliation, defeat, disempowerment and loss of dignity mainly through armed struggle. Palestine, for the past 60 years, and currently Afghanistan, Iraq and other simmering internal conflicts speak volumes about how uncritically the majority of Muslims have glorified reactive violence, not only as just but as the only effective way of getting wrongs righted.

The logic of violence is self-defeating and self-destructive; it leaves no winners, only generations of disorientated and misguided men and women. We have too many of them in Pakistan, a legacy of our follies in the Afghan wars. It is very difficult and even risky to argue against violence and violent religious, sectarian and ethnic groups, but for the sake of humanity and in the interests of Muslims and Pakistan, it has to be done.

Serious disagreement does exist on questions of power, legitimate government, constitutional action, rights violations and global justice. No doubt the only way to address them all is through legal, peaceful and non-violent means. This is a course that our religious and ethnic groups have refused to explore.

But one has to take into account not only the issue of the immorality of violent means but also the reality of modern states. The age of political romanticism about armed struggles and revolutions is long past, and there is no point in living in delusion. The only meaningful change would be incremental in nature, but can be accelerated through political consensus and collective social energy.

Pakistan has yet another chance to reshape itself according to a modernist, progressive vision, as the country struggles to make a transition to democracy. A moderate, liberal, democratic and forward-looking Pakistan would be a better place for Muslims and other citizens than a sectarian, strife-stricken and poverty-ridden Pakistan vulnerable to Taliban-type extremist movements. There are two clear paths before the Pakistani society — militancy or non-violence; one leads to hopelessness and self-destruction and the other to progress and modernity. The coming years will determine which path Pakistan is likely to take.

Conclusion

Taliban militancy and organised violence against the state and society present the most serious threat to national security. The grimness of this threat lies in its religious roots and radical worldview. The Taliban movement is a variant of political Islamism that has renounced democratic, constitutional and political paths to power and instead believes in the theory and practice of conquest in the image of medieval adventurists.

The problem is that the national and international atmosphere today is different. We now live in territorial nation-states and bounded political communities. The Taliban and their allied religious groups reject the territorial state and maintain transnational political and ideological links that spread across the globe. They have a mutual support system, sanctuaries and common sources of funding, and share a common vision and project of terrorising, defeating and replacing the present state structure, which in their view does not represent Islam or the "real" interests of Muslims. Their narrative of historic grievances against the local and global order and critique of the national ruling classes "naturally" facilitates their political communication with the disempowered, unskilled and unemployable youth in the socially and economically depressed regions of Pakistan.

Social structures that shape power relations, determine the social significance of individuals and groups and allocate political roles are neither just nor based on prudence and rationality. Dominant groups like the land-owning class, caste and tribal elites and the *gadinasheens* (hereditary elites owing power to holy shrines) have monopolised the social and political spaces of value. They could continue in their privileged positions, without a major challenge, were they to fulfil the role that similar conservative social groups in other societies have performed: being responsive to society and responsible in their exercise of power while pushing society forward through an emphasis on equity and equality.

Even members of the middle class, who play a subordinate role in the dynastic party system, have joined in the rapaciousness of the ruling groups. This does not send a message of hope to the disenfranchised youth and disillusioned social classes. The frustration of these classes has thus proved a fertile ground for the Taliban insurgency and Islamic radicalism.

Our focus on contemporary violence and its features should not divert our attention from the larger and more complex issue of the sociology of violence; the social conditions that promote and breed violent beliefs and practices.

As we have examined in this chapter, religious militancy in its many forms poses a grave challenge to the social harmony and national security of Pakistan. Much of the religious violence in the subcontinent and its more frequent eruption and persistence in Pakistan is rooted in the unarticulated but easily discernible form of religious fascism.

The rise of religious violence is both the consequence of internal mismanagement of economy and politics as well as a response to the perceived injustices to the Muslims in the region and beyond and their perceived repression by the powerful states. The question that we have raised and have tried to answer in this chapter is how discourse on Islam and weaknesses of the state have contributed to violence motivated by religious considerations. Religion, specifically Islam, since the launching of the Pakistan Movement, has been one of the primary tools of political mobilisation, and its social and political appeals continue to remain strong in some sections of the Pakistani society. The challenge Pakistan faces is where to situate religion in the state or in the society, and what can be the acceptable balance.

Chapter 7

Prospects for Conflict Resolutions in South Asia

Dayan Jayatilleka

South Asia is where I come from. It is one aspect of my identity. I am proud and pleased to be South Asian. In many gatherings I find that the South Asians perform very well. However, it is rare that they perform as a group, a collective (though I personally experienced the successful solidarity of South Asia at the United Nations Human Rights Council's special session on Sri Lanka this May). South Asia has so many commonalities and the elites of the South Asian countries have many interconnections that they easily feel at home in each other's company and in each other's countries, notwithstanding the state of inter-governmental relations. At social gatherings the interactions of South Asians are so cordial it is difficult to believe that many wars have been fought between these states. Little has been made of these commonalities and the potentiality of the region *qua* region remains almost wholly untapped.

The Blowback Zone

Instead, the region is synonymous with conflict. A few years ago, South Asia was identified as the most dangerous region on earth, though that has now been replaced by a definition that embeds South Asia in a larger Middle East or, to go back a decade earlier to Brzezinski's definition, a crescent of conflict.

The region contains almost every form of known conflict: intrastate and interstate; conflicts that arise from within the region, even intrastate conflicts, but which then go global, are globalised,

141

reaching out to other parts of the world and triggering military responses from afar, which in turn destabilise societies and states in the region. It is probably that area of the world in which the policies of the Cold War have had the worst consequences for their practitioners. South Asia has been the Blowback Zone.

For this reason alone, every effort must be made to seek out methods and mechanisms of conflict prevention, management, resolution and transformation.

Nowhere, it may be said, is greater potential thwarted by conflict. Though the Middle East runs a close second, where else in the world is there so wide a gap between the promise held by regional cooperation and the frustration of potential by the fact of conflict? This too makes it incumbent that the search for methods of conflict transformation be hastened. This search must be South Asian, not the burden or preserve of individual states and societies.

The varieties of armed political conflict in South Asia are roughly divisible into two standard varieties, intrastate and interstate, which as we shall later observe have a tendency to morph or merge in certain situations. The intrastate conflicts are themselves further divisible into socioeconomic conflicts and collective identity conflicts. By socioeconomic I refer to class or class-caste conflicts, those between rich and poor, haves and have-nots, or ideological conflicts based on appeals to these above-mentioned issues. These are also referred to as anti-systemic conflicts; those that call into question the totality of the system both locally and globally, and attempt a total overthrow of the system of socioeconomic and political power relations, and its replacement by an alternative, at least at the national level. By collective identity conflicts I refer to ethno-linguistic, ethno-religious or ethno-regional struggles. These do not attempt the overthrow or transformation of the system as a whole and its replacement by an alternative model. They often posit an exit from the system in the form of secession, resulting in the setting up of a state with a roughly similar socioeconomic system and power relations, or a drastic reform within the system along federal or autonomous lines.

The major identity-based conflicts have been the persistent ones in the extremities of India, its Northeast and Northwest, and the higher-intensity war in Sri Lanka which has had a dramatic denouement.

South Asia has witnessed more significant socioeconomic or anti-systemic ideological conflicts than most areas of the world outside of Southeast Asia and Latin America. Sri Lanka was the site of two Southern upheavals, in 1971 and 1986–1990, from within the majority ethnic community, led by the ultra-left, xenophobic Janatha Vimukthi Peramuna (JVP). Bangladesh had the radical-left-led military uprising of the Jatiyo Samajtantrik Dal (JSD) in the mid-1970s. While the most successful has been the Nepali Maoist insurgency, in a narrative that is as yet unfolding, the most portentous, potentially, if only because of its location, is India's Maoist insurgency which, as Prime Minister Manmohan Singh has recently noted, has a 40-year history and has seen a contemporary resurgence.

The radical insurgency has been shocking because of its persistence or renewal, but more so because India is the new model for the global South, combining high growth with secular democracy and quasi-federalism. It is regarded as a template for the politics of unity in diversity. According to theory, a radical revolutionary insurgency should not persist, still less expand, in the face of high growth and democracy. As we shall examine later in this chapter, the insurgency actually serves as an early warning sign of (social) systemic stress.

In Sri Lanka, a highly successful and historic victory has been obtained over one of the most internationally prominent terrorist armies or militia, the LTTE. So far there is no sign that this military victory will be followed by the successful building of a society in which conflict is pre-empted or skillfully managed. Indeed the character of the post-war process shows signs of a lapse into conflict which is not armed, but civic in nature.

In Nepal, the situation is opaque, with a Maoist party that is paradoxically far more sophisticated than those of the politically infinitely more evolved India, and is biding its time for a renewed surge which may be political, military or both. What happens in Nepal has strategic consequences far beyond its borders, most obviously in the ripple effects of the example it holds for the Maoist insurgency in India.

In Bangladesh, conflict is relatively marginal and in the Maldives seems absent due to the recent political transformations, except for a brief episode of Islamic fundamentalist terrorism.

This leaves Afghanistan and Pakistan, now referred to as one strategic unit or theatre, Af–Pak, which is not as absurd as it may seem, given that the conflict in one impacts so directly on the other. The interconnection with the conflict in Kashmir prompts me to suggest that it may not be inapposite to speak of a triad, Af–Pak–Kash, as a conflict "complex". A deeper examination reveals that this interconnectedness is perforated with contradictions and that moves which may be necessary in one part of this theatre undermines stability in another part.

At the level of interstate conflict, while there is occasional tension or friction on some borders, the main area of concern remains the Afghanistan–Pakistan–India triangle.

Let us now move from that overview to the prospects for conflict resolutions.

The intrastate anti-systemic conflicts in the region, again most dramatically exemplified by the Sri Lankan far-left insurgencies of 1971 and the late 1980s, are in decline or dormant with the important exceptions of the complicated dynamics in Nepal and the recrudescent and proliferating Maoist insurgency in India.

The Indian and Chinese Models and the Maoist Surge in South Asia Today

Nepal

Unlike the JVP and the LTTE of Sri Lanka, the Maoists of Nepal knew when to switch from armed struggle to negotiation, mass struggle and parliamentary politics. In short they were Leninists, had correctly calculated the conjuncture and changing correlation of forces, and mastered "all forms of struggle". Had the JVP and LTTE possessed a leadership with this same political literacy, education, clarity and maturity, neither Wijeweera nor Prabhakaran would be ignominiously dead, with their leadership core, military cadre and armed rebellions decimated.

Nepal today is reminiscent of Portugal in 1975–1976, a situation of virtual dual power which could go either way. In Portugal the revolutionaries were divided and not themselves armed, but their allies in the armed forces were. In Nepal, the armed forces have few revolutionary sympathisers, if any, but the revolutionary forces are themselves armed to some degree, despite the demilitarisation. The advance of the radical left in Portugal was thwarted by the revived power of the Social Democratic Left led by Mário Soares and the ambiguity of the pro-Moscow Communists led by Álvaro Cunhal. The revolution was itself a congeries of armed radical groupuscules or focus. In Nepal, however, though the Left is divided, there is a cohesive vanguard party with a national leader, Pushpakumar Dayal; there is no strong social democratic intermediary and one doubts whether the unarmed Left is able to play such a role. Above all, the relatively unchanged character of the land tenure system provides purchase for the Maoists. At the moment the situation is characterised by what Antonio Gramsci called catastrophic equilibrium — an equilibrium of forces tending towards catastrophe. The Maoists seem readier to take the initiative, and given the seemingly zero-sum nature of the issue in dispute, the character of the armed forces and control over them, it may be impossible to avoid another bout of armed or politico-military conflict in which Pushpakumar Dayal may return to his nom de guerre Comrade Prachanda (Comrade Violence). Compromise arrangements regarding the armed forces during transitions in Latin America, for instance in Nicaragua when the Sandinistas were vacating the seats of power in 1990, should be urgently studied for possible solutions to this impending conflict, at the heart of which is of course the question of whether the assumption of power by the Maoists has a teleological inevitability, as they seem to believe, and whether the only route will be that of elections and respect for the democratic institutional and state order. To gain acceptability and legitimacy though, that order, which has not yet crystallised, will have to be thoroughly negotiated and agreed upon by consensus, with neither side — the revolutionaries nor the establishment politicians and classes — attempting a unilateral push forward or rollback, i.e. an insurrection or a putsch, using armed force. At the moment, the prospects for such a peaceful resolution are few and will remain so unless there is sustained South Asian engagement.

India

The issue of resolving India's growing Maoist insurgency brings us to a cluster of crucial problems and debates, not least a comparison of the Indian and Chinese development miracles, their respective futures, the prospects of each to function as a model, and the potential global role of each of these emergent Asian powers. Those who bet on India hold that the Indian political system, with its combination of multi-party democracy and quasi-federalism, provides greater long-term sustainability and a guarantee of success for the Indian model, while China's regulated, regimented or closed political system constitutes an Achilles' heel in terms of the management of contradictions. The contrary view holds that it is precisely China's political system that permits the management of social and political contradictions in a manner that contains fissiparous tendencies and makes for long-term stability while India's multiple contradictions could smolder and ignite into Naipaul's "million mutinies".

While the jury will remain out for quite some time on this debate, the reactivation and rapid proliferation of India's Maoist insurgency does shed light on the weak link of India's development. That weak link or the weakest of those links is not in Kashmir or the Northeast, but in the Indian socioeconomic formation itself. Asymmetric warfare in India follows the fault lines and fissures of India's asymmetric development. Those fault lines are social or socioeconomic and stem from the problem of the extremely uneven development of India's capitalism.

Sixty years after the founding of the People's Republic, it is possible to discern the most important continuities between the Maoist and post-Maoist periods. This is not only the obvious one of the continuing rule of the Communist party, but a deeper, less apparent one. I refer to the fact that the massive radical agrarian revolution of Mao has laid the foundation for successful industrialisation — some might say capitalist development — of China. This is perhaps the longer-term strength of the Chinese model, just as its non-revolutionary, even counter-revolutionary variant has been key to the Southeast Asian success stories of South Korea and Taiwan. India, by contrast, has experienced a development miracle while not having resolved the agrarian question; the question of archaic systems of land tenure; the question of the persistence of a class of large landowners who engage in coercive social control; and the related question of caste oppression or the peculiar combination of class and caste.

If one were to use the schema of the bourgeois democratic revolution, be it in its Marxian version or that of Barrington Moore, it is possible to conclude that both India and China have fulfilled the tasks of national unification, though that is not without its challenges at their peripheries. However, while India has set up a democratic republic in the political sphere, which is one of the tasks and targets of the so-called bourgeois revolutions, it has not completed its agrarian or rural accompaniment. China on the other hand has, though it has obviously eschewed the setting up of a bourgeois democratic republic. Thus India has completed the political but not the social aspect of the classic bourgeois democratic revolution while it is arguably the other way round in the case of China. India's capitalist development more closely approximates the path of Tsarist Russia or the Prussian path, rather than the American path, if one may use the typology pioneered by the young Lenin in his *The Development of Capitalism in Russia*. It is India's advanced political system that has prevented a system-wide crisis resulting from this socioeconomic unevenness. However, that political system has been unable to prevent the persistence and progress of the Maoist rural insurgency.

A scenario of the countrywide or even statewide seizure of power by the Indian Maoists is wildly improbable. India is heavily industrial and modern while the insurgency is not. The maximum it may be able to achieve is the combination of a rural spread with urban guerrilla attacks such as those during the Naxalite insurgency of the late 1960s and early 1970s or the Peruvian Shining Path guerrilla experience. The very existence of a strong electoral democratic system and a trade unionist Left, the CPI-M and the CPI, guarantees the failure of the Maoist insurgency in terms of its ultimate objective. However, the problems that it feeds off, namely rural backwardness and caste oppression, coupled with the radical insurgency that these fuel, and the escalating costs of counter-insurgency could have a cumulative and growing drag effect on the Indian economic miracle. Given the vastness of the Indian population, that drag effect could cause system-wide dissonance if it slows down India's growth over time.

The prospects for conflict resolution in India depend on the readiness of its political class to engage in sweeping agrarian reforms which would in turn mean a realignment of sociopolitical forces in the countryside. Already where the BJP is strong, the landlord classes feel freer to engage in violence against the poorer peasantry and subaltern castes, which in turn triggers a response from the Maoists. The challenge is before the Congress as to whether it can spearhead a thoroughgoing reform and modernisation of India's rural social and ideological relations. The hope and the irony is that India already has the ideas and concepts necessary for the task, Amartya Sen being only the best known to argue for the necessity and feasibility of combining growth, equity and democracy.

AF–PAK: The Stakes and Options in Afghanistan

From a global point of view there can be little doubt the Afghanistan–Pakistan–India triangle is the most decisive in South Asia, for the obvious reason that two of these three states are nuclear armed. It is true that the Indo–Pak relationship has been relatively stable and that this stability has been mightily assisted by the diplomacy of the United States during moments of tension such as the Kargil crisis. This diplomatic adhesive has been strengthened by the new style and approach of President Barack Obama. It is no less true that the Indo–Pakistani nuclear equation has not achieved the degree of depth and stability that the US–USSR relationship had acquired during the Cold War, and one may envisage a scenario in which more ideologically charged governments come into office in both Pakistan and India, per-haps in reaction to one another, and set off an escalation of tensions which bring the two states to the brink. However, since this is not an imminent prospect I shall not dwell on it and prefer to move on to the more strikingly sensitive current theatre, the so-called Af–Pak area.

As an entry point, let me use an old question which has assumed the status of a cliché: Is Afghanistan, which was Russia's Vietnam, going to be America's second Vietnam? Is the United States going to suffer the same fate as Russia in Afghanistan?

On one level the answer is clearly no. The USSR was already suffering serious internal stagnation and decay, and while the United States is in grave economic difficulty, there is no evidence of any weakness which can result in systemic implosion. When the USSR entered Afghanistan it had long lost its ideological vitality while the United States under President Obama has clearly regained its own. The United States was able to create a quagmire for the USSR by securing the support of a wide coalition of disparate forces, ranging from China to Saudi Arabia and, most importantly, Pakistan. It provided the Afghan insurgents the means — Stinger missiles — to neutralize Soviet airpower. By contrast, the only coalition that exists today, however skimpy, is one supportive of the United States. There is no state, neighbouring or further afield, that supports the insurgency. Even a regime with which the United States has serious contradictions, Iran, does not seek to undermine US policy in Afghanistan.

Perhaps most importantly there are the twin factors of the nature of the insurgent leadership itself and the period of history in which the struggle takes place. The Vietnamese were led by Ho Chi Minh and the Vietnamese Communist Party, a tough-minded and brilliant leadership capable of the most sophisticated understanding of the world and possessed of a mastery of strategy and tactics ranging from small-unit and large-scale battles to the negotiations in Paris. The Taliban simply is not in the same class. At its most starkly personal, Ho Chi Minh and Le Duan were more than a match for Lyndon Johnson and Richard Nixon while Mullah Omar and Osama bin Laden is hardly the intellectual equal, still less superior, of Barack Obama. While North Vietnam was itself a state which functioned as a rear base for the Southern guerrillas and, later, conventional units operating in the South, the Vietnamese Communists were able to count on the support of either the USSR or the People's Republic of China, using their rivalry to secure support from both or at least one. The Taliban has no state which constitutes a rear base. The Vietnamese fought their war when Communism or Socialism was a truly global contender, while the Taliban's brand of radical Islam is not a truly global contender in that this ideology is culturally circumscribed and is not universalist in its appeal. By contrast the Vietnamese had tens of thousands of youngsters in the West, educated at the best of Western universities, chanting slogans in favour of the Viet Cong and waving portraits of Uncle Ho, while it is unthinkable that Osama bin Laden or Mullah Omar would have such a resonance within Western societies.

Still there are disturbing possibilities that the experience of the United States in Afghanistan could resemble its experience in Vietnam. On the ground, the war is not being won. The US economy may be unable to risk an escalation of American commitment in terms of far more troops for a far longer period. US public opinion may well flag. If so, the Taliban, which is unable to beat the United States on the battlefield and score anything like a Dien Bien Phu or even a Tet offensive, may be able to secure the same result as in Vietnam: a US withdrawal through sheer fatigue. If so the consequences are incalculable. Perhaps as in the case of Vietnam the dominoes will *not* fall and the fallout will be absorbable. Or perhaps the opposite will be at least partially true and Islamic radicals, whatever their sectarian differences, will feel emboldened by their victory, considering it evidence of the weakening of the moral fibre of liberal democracies and the decline of the sole superpower, the United States, signalling God-given sanction for endless jihad. This may in turn undermine the political fortunes of liberalism in the West, especially in the United States, and aid the recovery of the Right, with all the polarising consequences this holds for world politics. Whichever way it goes, failure in Afghanistan may impact upon the future of the Obama presidency. If so, it may have a knock-on effect on US relations with the rest of the world, which have improved dramatically under the Obama presidency. Yet, how is one to define failure? Is it withdrawal or a continued stay in a quagmire? More importantly, how will the US electorate, or the majority of it, define failure?

How will victory and defeat each impact on Pakistan and Indian Kashmir? The surge of force levels, drone strikes and casualties inflicted on the Taliban in the event of victory could either stabilise or radicalise areas and social sectors of Pakistan. Conversely, an American military failure in Afghanistan could have the impact of further motivating and emboldening militancy in that state, and in Indian Kashmir, heightening threat perceptions in India.

What then are the prospects of conflict resolution? President Obama has so far seen the Afghan war, in contradistinction to the one in Iraq, as a necessary war, in an echo of Machiavelli's dictum that the only just war is a necessary war. It would perhaps be prudent on his part to avoid the main mistake of Donald Rumsfeld which was the under commitment of troops, and to observe the fundaments of the Powell doctrine of deploying sufficiently large force levels if a particular war is deemed a necessary one.

Militarily the situation necessitates a pincer action from the Afghan and Pakistani fronts, with a degree of coordination that has yet to be witnessed. The political consequences, if not managed, could be counterproductive. While the recent military offensive by the Pakistani army in the Swat valley has been a relative success with little visible political blowback, and the handling of the internally displaced has been vastly better than that in Sri Lanka, public opinion polls reveal that at the level of the Pakistani people, a broad consensus must be constructed. How to involve and yet insulate Pakistan is the dilemma. The stabilisation of the Pakistani factor requires drawing in the two major Pakistani political formations led by the two preeminent figures, President Zardari and Nawaz Sharif. Given the zero-sum nature of politics in South Asia (outside, arguably, of India), this seems as impossible as it is imperative. Perhaps it is the Obama administration that can play a productive role here, but US involvement may make the process radioactive on the Pakistani street.

This makes it impossible for me to resist the temptation to make two suggestions, one out-of-the-box, and the other, possibly heretical, as to how the situation in Afghanistan may be stabilised and possibly turned around.

The first is that the Obama administration should take a second look at and seek to bolster the South Asian Association for Regional Cooperation (SAARC) as a rearguard and counterweight to the spread of extremism, and a regional body which, in augmented form, may be able to play a stabilising role in Afghanistan. An active US role may be able to better manage and balance the structural asymmetries of SAARC which have had a dysfunctional, even debilitating effect.

The second suggested step, the heretical one, derives from my perception of the essential problem which seems to me to be the thinness of the human resource base of the state. The state lacks a qualified cadre. The irony is that there are pools of potential cadre who are educated and professionally trained, share the same ideals of the education of women and broad social modernisation as the US administration, and, more dramatically, have a proven resistance to the siren song of radical Islamic militancy. These are the scattered, exiled cadre of the PDPA, the party of the Afghan revolution of 1978, with its notorious fratricidal factions, the Khalq and the Parcham, whose internecine strife probably cost them state power. These cadres are scattered in parts of the former Soviet space, in India and even Pakistan. They are in no shape to attempt any political adventures, now that the Cold War is over, global socialism has collapsed, the USSR is no more, history has moved on and their very existence would depend on US power. They are far more likely to be Obama fans than anything else! I am not arguing for their reinstatement in power but for their reincorporation and reintegration into the Afghan state and society in what Enrico Berlinguer, the father of Eurocommunism, used to call a "*compromesso storico*", a "historic compromise". With many even less savoury precedents in the post-World War II period, this strategy is a low-risk, (potentially) high-yield one, which can "thicken" the state with trained, educated, middle-class professionals, expanding the core of an anti-Taliban modernising coalition.

This is but a domestic corollary — may I say, the *missing* domestic corollary — and concomitant with President Obama's regionalised approach to the Afghan crisis and his attempt at broadening the international alliance supporting the anti-Al-Qaeda/Taliban effort.

While I am not unmindful of the possible blowback, I would still maintain that, if carefully handled, the move I suggest here can be a "game-changer" in a positive sense.

Undergirding my suggestion is the hypothesis that in the longer view of history, the Soviet intervention in Afghanistan may be seen not only as an ideological or strategic move, defensive, preemptive or offensive, by the USSR in a Cold War context, but as a battle by a form of modernity against a resurgence of the premodern or archaic. In that sense the Soviet and US efforts can be seen as part of a (civilisational?) continuum. Of course this presupposes that the Cold War itself is understood, at least in part, as a fratricidal civil war within modernity; between two alternative projects, one of which won.

Let me conclude this section of my chapter by signalling alarm about an "outlier", a factor which could upset many equations. I refer to a possible Israeli attack on Iran. I believe that it is unlikely that there will be a US strike, but I also fear that Israel will launch an attack, not least with the hope of upsetting the political equation in the United States and limiting President Obama to a single term. The new Israeli administration may calculate that an attack on Iran and a retaliatory Iranian strike could create a situation in which President Obama can be pressurised to act for fear of being outflanked by the Republican Right. If this takes place, there will be ripple effects throughout the Islamic world, irrespective of which sect or tendency of Islam each society preponderantly belongs to. The United States will also find a practical problem of overstretch which will affect its ability to function in Afghanistan. This in turn may be the Black Swan event that provides the Taliban and Al-Qaeda with their moment. Thus all bets are off in the event of an attack on Iran. Will the first black president of the United States be undone by a Black Swan event?

Sri Lanka's Lessons for the World

The second part of this chapter is devoted to the Sri Lankan experience of, and further prospects for, conflict resolution in my country. It is subdivided into two parts. The first part deals with Sri Lanka's experiences in conflict resolution, and the second part with the future prospects. I offer Sri Lanka's experiences not because I am unmindful that the thrust of this conference and the expectation from my paper is a forward-looking one, but because I think that Sri Lanka's conflict was so high-profile and complex that our experience could, if correctly comprehended, impact upon other states in South Asia, in the twin senses that a repetition of our errors could retard prospects for conflict resolution, while the adoption of our successes — if only where relevant and adaptable — could enhance and accelerate prospects for resolving and transforming conflicts.

The Sri Lankan effort at conflict resolution involved successive administrations of varying ideological persuasions, centre-right and centre-left. It also involved, at various times, a major regional player, India and a European small power, Norway. (Both attempts failed due to perceptions of partiality, and should be closely scrutinised as case studies so as to enhance the theory and practice of third-party efforts at conflict resolution.) Sri Lanka's conflict entailed policies ranging from a pure military approach to a ceasefire and extensive concessions, through various mixes which gave predominance to either the military or the political. Finally the conflict in its armed form was terminated by classical military means. However, the underlying ethno-regional tensions and contradictions remain, unaddressed in some parts, heightened in others, and modified by the war in other parts of the problem. This can lead to the recrudescence of the conflict, not so much in its armed form, which can be easily handled by the Sri Lankan armed forces whatever its intensity, but by civic conflict, which cannot be handled by such means without risk of permanent strife. This is not to dilute the enormous achievement of the Sri Lankan state, society and armed forces in crushing a terrorist armed force which was one of the best known brand names in the business. What is required is, among other things, an understanding of the specificity of the Sri Lankan achievement and the limits of its relevance and possible application. Its adoption will require considerable local adaptation.

When the insurgency was at the stage that it might have been split and undermined by reforms, the obduracy of political parties and leaders claiming to speak for the Sinhala majority forestalled such reform. At a subsequent stage, the insurgency had grown to the point that it was dominated and then violently monopolised by the most extremist and fanatical organisation. This became the main factor that precluded any serious reform, though by then the state was "walking on two legs", as Chairman Mao would have it, striving to combine political reform with military offensives. In the third stage, the administration adopted a policy of unilateral concessions, which its opponents within the state and without, denounced as a policy of appeasement. Even such a policy failed to thaw the insurgent movement, which was unwilling to settle for anything less than *de facto* separation and that too as a halfway house to *de jure* independence, openly proclaiming and inwardly believing that it could beat the state forces in any confrontation while deterring any significant external support for the state. In its final phase, the separatist insurgency had grown to the level of a contending armed force but without the undergirding, organic support structures necessary for a guerrilla force to move to stage three of the Mao–Giap schema. This provided the Sri Lankan state with the opportunity of a full-on multi-front military offensive and to defeat the Tigers in a classic denouement.

The main lessons then are, in the form of 13 theses, the following:

Thesis I   Early reforms may undercut the momentum of an insurgency; delayed ones will not.

Thesis II   The success of efforts at conflict resolution depends crucially on the intrinsic character of the armed non-state actor in question. One size does not fit all.

Thesis III Distinctions must be drawn between terrorist movements and armed resistance movements, as well as between rational albeit extremist/radical organisations and non-rational, fanatical or fundamentalist ones.

Thesis IV   Further differentiations must be made with regard to the stage of growth of the armed struggle and the character of the organisation that exercises fluid or entrenched hegemony or monopoly within that struggle.

Thesis V   Military action must not be the first resort or the main aspect of policy in the first instance, though a security component may be needed to effect and safeguard reforms.

Thesis VI   However, if the armed struggle is monopolised by a fanatical organisation which violates humanitarian norms and resorts persistently to terrorism (defined as the intentional or witting targeting of noncombatants), then the military factor in the state's response must perforce acquire greater importance.

Thesis VII   The political, social and military tracks of a multi-track strategy must not undermine each other; they must demonstrate policy coherence and converge on a clear strategic goal.

Thesis VIII   In the case of an armed struggle that has grown to the point of large-unit conventional or semi-conventional combat, it must be recognised as a war and must be fought as such.

Thesis IX   The objective of such a war could either be the defeat of the enemy or driving it to a negotiated settlement that is balanced, mutual, reciprocal and verifiable, rather than a breathing space for rearming, regrouping and renewal of the insurgency.

Thesis X   Third-party efforts at conflict resolution must not depend solely or primarily on those states which have ethnic constituencies, indigenous or immigrant, drawn from only one of the belligerents. Though such states may be the ones to be automatically drawn in, and therefore most strongly motivated to play a role with its attendant risks, such embedded lobbies of co-ethnics in a zero-sum situation will vitiate attempts at conflict resolution because the intermediary will not be perceived as a neutral umpire, and there will be a backlash. Ideally the mediating/intervening state should have, in its make-up, no correlative reflecting the conflict, or should fairly evenly represent all the belligerent communities, or should be a regional coalition which collectively neutralises the profile of unevenness in the composition of any one state.

Thesis XI   In the extreme case of an insurgency that is dominated or monopolised by a terrorist and or fanatical organisation and has grown to the level of a war, the objective of state policy must be, and indeed can be, nothing other than the military defeat of the enemy, the destruction of its military apparatus, the neutralisation of its leadership and the recovery of all terrain lost to it, in short, "the annihilation of the living forces of the enemy" as the world's greatest living strategist, Vietnam's General Vo Nguyen Giap, put it.

Thesis XII   Such a war must not be punctuated by ceasefires and negotiations which debilitate the morale of the armed forces.

Thesis XIII In the case of an outcome of the decisive military defeat of the enemy, sociopolitical reforms could parallel but must at least follow the military victory and do so swiftly. If not, there could either be a reactivation of the insurgency or the permanent alienation of a section of the citizenry which either supported or came under the influence of the armed struggle or belong to the same social constituency from which it sprang and share the insurgents' sense of collective grievance.

Prospects for durable peace

The most intense and high-profile aspect of the Sri Lankan conflict has just been resolved: the deadly conflict; the mid-intensity war. What remains is the postwar crisis, the delay or inability to reap the peace dividend by making the transition to a stable and just framework for durable peace and successful nation building.

There are three axial routes of the Lankan crisis or three pillars between which Lankan political development takes place and the crisis continues. I refer to three thematic problems or issue clusters, namely that of the *North-South axis*, the ethno-national question, of power sharing between the centre and periphery or the constituent communities of the island; the *rich-poor axis*, the socioeconomic question, that between the haves and have-nots, the elites and the mass; and the *country-world axis*, that of the island and its relationships with the world. The first and third issues are to do with various dimensions of identity, internal and external.

It is my settled conviction that none of these three problems can be successfully addressed without addressing the other two. An attempt to resolve the ethno-national without sensitivity to mass deprivation and nationalist or patriotic sentiment only makes that attempt vulnerable to a populist or plebian backlash. This is also why I am of the view that neither an *elitist neoliberal cosmopolitanism* nor the *neoconservative populism* that is currently the dominant Lankan ideology will be able to resolve the problem of reconciling Sri Lanka's collective identities. That will require a *centrist, social democratic or progressive liberal* perspective rather like that of India's Congress Party or the US Democrats.

The crux of the issue was most pithily stated in 1926 by the young SWRD Bandaranaike (who, ironically enough, was to be the Prime Minister who introduced the controversial Sinhala-only policy 30 years later), when he warned prophetically of impending crisis, pointing out that a centralised form of state presupposes a homogeneous society while no society anywhere in the world as "communally" heterogeneous as that of Ceylon has, to his knowledge, successfully sustained a centralised state form. In sum, the young Bandaranaike pointed out the dysfunctional asymmetry between the "base" or "substructure", the underlying social formation of the island with its polyethnic mosaic, and a centralised political "superstructure".

This contradiction remains unresolved eight decades after its embryonic articulation by him, but it does not remain unaltered. Inasmuch as the recently concluded Thirty Years War arose out of this contradiction and insofar as that war ended in the decisive victory of one side, the state, and defeat and destruction of the other, the underlying contradiction itself cannot but be drastically altered by the new politico-military balance of forces in which the strategic military hegemony of the state is, in all probability, unassailable. However, the decisive and, to my mind, wholly welcome military defeat of the LTTE can alter the contradiction but cannot abolish it. Sri Lankan society seems divided between those who assert that the underlying problem remains despite the outcome of the war and those who claim that the problem itself has been resolved or effaced. Too few seem to transcend these dual dogmatisms to comprehend that there is a complex mix of continuity and change, the ratio of which is difficult to determine: the problem remains, but has changed; the problem has changed, but remains.

One of the fundamental aspects of the Sri Lankan crisis today is a government that is alienated from the minorities and an opposition that is alienated from the majority. A majoritarian approach cannot sustain, while a minoritarian approach cannot succeed.

There seems to be an assumption that it is inherently contradictory to wage a war *and* push for reforms such as devolution of power. The notion that waging a necessary war against terrorism and the implementation of reforms are inherently contradictory posits a dangerously dogmatic dichotomy shared by the neoliberal pacifists and the neoconservative populists. Realists (Russia's Putin) know that a successful strategy against separatist terrorism organically links devolution — power sharing with the local community or local allies — with a military campaign, whether devolution precedes, parallels or follows military victory.

There are three alternatives out there in the discussion on postwar Sri Lanka. The first is *accommodation on the basis of power sharing*, or what I call the Chechen model (to the accompaniment of much shuddering among liberals) or the Putin model. This involves a full-on military offensive to destroy separatist terrorism, followed by a modest but very real local autonomy and rule of the liberated or re-taken area through partnership with the local leaders (or what a cynic might call local proxies). The second model is that of *equal assimilation*, assimilation which can be successful only on the basis of equality of citizenship and non-discrimination, in which the Sri Lankan Constitution changes in such a manner that no community, be it ethnic, linguistic or religious, has a constitutionally entrenched privilege. The third model is of *occupation*; of unequal assimilation at the centre and internal colonialism at the periphery. I am not saying that the Sri Lankan state is attempting this. What I am saying is that these are the ideological options out there in society. I for one do not consider the third option to be diplomatically viable or strategically sustainable.

Why has there been no peace dividend? It is not only because of the global economic downturn but because we have not overcome the policy landmines that lie between us and that peace dividend. These policy landmines and roadblocks have not been removed because they are not seen as roadblocks but as desirable by some sectors of the power bloc and the ruling coalition.

This brings us to a more crucial question: Why are we in a post-war crisis? Because we are deadlocked as to the direction in which we want to head and the destination we wish to get to. There is no informed open discussion about the nature of the postwar order.

This too is only one aspect of the matter. The truth is that we are agreed with the unstated proposition of "Never Again", by which is meant that there should never again be a separatist challenge and that our military victory must be irreversible. The predominant, if invisible, subterranean perspective in the state and (Southern/Sinhala) society seems to be that Tamil separatism should not only be uprooted but that the soil in which its seeds may germinate should be upturned. This view is one of permanent rollback and counter-reformation, targeting or diluting even the 13th amendment to the Constitution (resulting from the Indo–Lanka Accord of 1987) which gives limited autonomy to the provinces, and redrawing the map of the North and the East. It is a hard-line neoconservative perspective.

There is a contrary view, which is that Tamil separatism can be preempted only by a more liberal approach which goes beyond the 13th amendment to explore federal or quasi-federal alternatives.

To both these approaches there is an alternative third approach, which is one I hold, hopefully not in isolation. This is a policy mix that recognises the need for a long-term and secure military presence in those areas as well as certain security red lines, which however must be broadly parametric rather than narrowly prescriptive, strictly professional rather than ethno-religious. This recognition is coupled with another, namely that Tamil nationalism cannot be stamped out and that if there is a perceived threat to their collective identity we shall face blowback. This may not take the form of a renewed insurgency, which our military can handle easily, but a civic conflict, which it cannot and must not be forced to. Sri Lanka does not enjoy the super-power umbrella that Israel does, and the recent remarks and moves by the US, UK, EU and UN together with the visit of MPs from neighbouring Tamil Nadu demonstrates that our treatment of the Tamils is under international scrutiny (partly driven by the Tamil diaspora). Therefore, we must combine security measures with political devolution within a unitary state, and improvement on the human rights and humanitarian fronts. This is a realist approach.

Sri Lanka's postwar crisis is one of the inability, unwillingness or delay in making the transition from a just war (in content if not always in method) to a just peace. Had we done so, there would be no crisis. There are those who will say that we cannot make the transition because the war was not just and that the absence of a just peace is evidence of the unjust character of the war. This is simply untrue. The Sri Lankan Final War 2006–2009 met all the criteria of a just war as did those waged against the Tigers from 1987 onwards. The Six-Day War of 1967 provides the classic example of a just war which failed to move on to a just peace.

In a related feature, the postwar crisis also results from the divergence of external and internal pressures and the state's inability to balance optimally and successfully between the two. External realities — not only the EU but more importantly the US, not only the West but also India — will not let the state implement a West Bank model in the North. The state feels it cannot eschew such a closed model and the drive towards it, because of hard-line domestic pressure groups which form part of the constituency of the ruling coalition. Failing to chart a middle path and balance between these contending forces, the state finds itself deadlocked.

A distinguished Sri Lankan archaeologist and former ambassador to UNESCO, Prof. Senaka Bandaranaike discerns a pattern in Sri Lankan history of sometimes being ahead of the rest of the subcontinent but never being able to achieve a decisive breakthrough and sustain it. This happened at least three times, he once said in a lecture I attended. Sri Lanka now has a second chance. It is as if we have obtained a second independence, the first when we were ahead of the game in the rest of Asia but then blew it. Let us hope we do not not blow it yet again.

Sri Lanka cannot defend its sovereignty against all comers from all points of the compass, North and South, West and East. Sovereignty not only has to be asserted, it has to be defended and defensible. It can defend its sovereignty only by power balancing in a multi-polar world. Starkly put, if we lose India, we lose even the Non-Aligned Movement and (as we saw in 1987 when Delhi dramatically impinged) we would be left naked.

This brings us to the impact of co-ethnics in a neighbouring state and overseas (in the so-called diaspora) as factors in complicating conflict resolution. Seventy million Tamils will not go away from the demographic make-up of India; a significant percentage of them will always be concerned about the fate of their ethnic kin in Sri Lanka, constituting a political factor that no government at the centre will ignore. Furthermore, no government at the centre will risk a significant degree of alienation of Tamil Nadu from the centre, on the basis that the latter does not care about the fate of Sri Lanka's Tamils. Sri Lankan Sinhalese could very well argue that it is none of their or anybody else's business but our own, but that is just not the way the world works. As a respected Sri Lankan journalist and editor Mervyn de Silva wrote, "in the age of identity, ethnicity walks on water". Look at the intervention or counter-intervention of Russia on behalf of the South Ossetians in the face of Georgian action (of which the perfect precursor was the Indian conduct of 1987).

My unit of analysis is the world system taken as single whole, a complex unevenly structured totality, and this is all the more relevant now that we are faced with the threat of a global protracted struggle with Tamil secessionism, driven by the Tamil diaspora. If the battlefield is global, the analysis cannot be purely local. Sri Lanka's sovereignty must be defended mainly by its own efforts, but cannot be defended solely or exclusively by them, and must be defended by a broad united front or concentric circles of alliances.

While Tamil separatism must be overcome, Sinhala and Tamil nationalism have to be contained if the country is to build a Sri Lankan national identity and consciousness. They can be contained only by being accommodated to some degree. Tamil nationalism can be contained only by a sufficiency of devolved power and resources. We must share power with one another so as to build a nation with and for us all.

Power sharing as solution

No devolution or too little, and communities will break away. Too much devolution and they will do the same. The degree of devolution at the periphery depends on the character of the mainstream. If one implements a strictly secular Republicanism as does France, and one is a French citizen with equal rights irrespective of ethnicity, then the need for substantive devolution at the periphery is virtually non-existent (though Corsica would doubtless disagree). However, if a society insists that the culture, language and civilisation of its majority must have some built-in preference, as is the case in Sri Lanka, then it is unrealistic to expect that those who do not belong to that culture but are inhabitants of the country would feel themselves fully integrated and un-alienated citizens. Full integration can only take place on the basis of full equality, and a citizenship that is blind to ethnic origin, religion and language. If the state and citizenship are not blind or even-handed but biased, then it is unavoidable that there will be demands by minorities for their own political space at the periphery. A moderate, rational political programme containing a progressive vision for Sri Lanka's postwar future is a necessary component for bringing this conflict to a successful close.

Xenophobia, cultural or otherwise, is profoundly counterproductive for winning the peace. Scholarly and scientific research has shown that creativity and innovation in all fields take place not so much from within the bowels of homogeneous and unchanging cultures but precisely where cultures interface, interact, exchange and cross-fertilise. Sir Arthur C. Clarke correctly observed that Sri Lanka contains the greatest cultural diversity in the most compressed space, which is a source of conflict but potentially also of great creativity. Unless we embrace pluralism, learn to celebrate the treasure that is our own diversity, and tap into it as an energy source for advance, we shall certainly be unable to compete regionally or globally. Worst of all we shall not be using all our cultural capacities, making the best of our endowments, making the best of ourselves.

If ideologies of resentment and closure prevail over those of conciliation and openness, Sri Lanka will be unable to manage the problem of the haemorrhage of quality human resources, which in turn will decide whether we shall develop or decline as a country.

Having won the war, Sri Lanka can lose the peace by one of two errors. The first would be to permit the separatist project to continue to function, for separatist political agencies to function unchecked. We could thus peacefully jeopardise that which the armed forces have won on the battlefield. This could generate a seriously destabilising nationalist-populist backlash. The equal and opposite error would be a lack of generosity, flexibility, enlightenment and wisdom, due to which we fail to expeditiously remove the discrimination, frustration and alienation felt by the Tamil minority. That would cause the reactivation, in one way or another, of the Tamil separatist struggle. Either outcome would betray the gains of military victory and continue to torment us.

The Obama paradigm

Speaking to the 200,000-strong crowd in Berlin's Tiergarten on July 24, 2008, Presidential Candidate Barack Obama said:

> …The walls between races and tribes; natives and immigrants; Christian and Muslim and Jew cannot stand. These now are the walls we must tear down.
>
> …Our allegiance has never been to any particular tribe or kingdom — indeed, every language is spoken in our country; every culture has left its imprint on ours; every point of view is expressed in our public squares. What has always united us — what has always driven our people; what drew my father to America's shores — is a set of ideals that speak to aspirations shared by all people: that we can live free from fear and free from want; that we can speak our minds and assemble with whomever we choose and worship as we please.

Obama points the way for Sinhalese, Tamils and Muslims. For the Tamils, the relevance and example should be clear: abandon projects of separatist walling-off, integrate into the mainstream, fight against discrimination and for equal rights, regard oneself as a Sri Lankan and compete as one. The African-Americans experienced slavery and segregation and still encounter racism, but Barack Obama's example is to transcend that experience, which was historically far worse than anything suffered by Tamils. His is the model of our martyred Foreign Minister Lakshman Kadirgamar, an ethnic Tamilian (whose oration for devolution in the Parliamentary Debate on the August 2000 Draft Constitution is cunningly ignored by Sinhalese chauvinists). It could come to the forefront only now that Kadirgamar's assassins, the Tigers, lie defeated.

What is the lesson and example for the Sinhalese? Barack Obama, perhaps the most intellectually gifted politician in today's world and potentially a philosopher-president in the Platonic sense, ushers in a new model of cultural globalisation and globalised culture of and for the 21st century. He is the modern, multiethnic, multicultural man, emerging from the melting-pot meritocracy that is America. However, this is not an exclusively American dream. It is not essentially different from the multiracialism of Cuba's Fidel Castro and South Africa's Nelson Mandela, or that of Jawaharlal Nehru, without whose inclusive, pluralist, secular, rational, modern leadership vision for an ancient, culturally rich society, India would not be the Asian success story and the 21st century miracle it has become.

Some states and societies are a hybrid, such as India, which has a secular Constitution, a pluralist society (the Prime Minister is a Sikh, the most powerful politician is of Italian origin, the most powerful political family is mixed-race), but also provides sufficient space for its constituent communities in the form of a quasi-federal system and linguistic states.

Sri Lanka is far from a situation in which society is integrated, discrimination is aggressively tackled and the state is neutral between communities. In such a context, where one individual is not the equal of the other and one community has more privileges than the other, it is the case the world over that collectivities with their distinctive identities and inhabiting recognisable geographic areas over long periods tend to seek some political space and measure of self-rule/ self-governance. I cannot think of any state in the world, and at the

UN in Geneva I worked among 193, that does not hold that Sri Lanka's Tamils deserve and require equal rights in practice, as well as some autonomous political space, be it devolution of power to autonomous regions or provinces (as in Britain or China) or something more.

A result of the Indo–Sri Lanka Accord of 1987, the 13th amendment to the Constitution of Sri Lanka makes for the devolution of power and provincial autonomy within a unitary framework. It is the most modest and economical of these arrangements as far as the majority goes. Even purely domestic political accommodation between the communities/ethnic collectivities is impossible other than on the basis of the 13th amendment at the minimum.

Full if graduated implementation of the 13th amendment, i.e. the fullest possible devolution of powers within our Constitution, is an essential part of the minimum political programme on which such a global united front can be built and sustained.

Prabhakaran took a grave risk and waged his second war, this time against the Indian peacekeeping force, because he knew that provincial autonomy as envisaged in the Indo–Lanka Accord and contained in the 13th amendment a year later was a death trap for Tamil secessionism. This is because authentic moderate reform is a death trap for extremism anywhere, anytime.

There is nothing that the Tiger international network and the pro-Tiger, pro-Tamil Eelam Tamil diaspora would like better, than to see a gap open up in the partnership between Sri Lanka and India; a gap that they will seek to manipulate in consonance with their Western patrons and friends. The non-implementation of the 13th amendment will open up such a gap.

Why compromise on the basis of the 13th amendment, ask the extremists on both sides of the ethnic divide. The answer is that anything else would be too risky. Open up the issue again and the Sinhalese may offer less, the Tamils may ask for more and the world may see an even more divided island.

Historically this is the best time to effect a political reconciliation between the Sinhala and Tamil communities in Sri Lanka. If we do not do so internally, space opens for external interference. If a minority anywhere in the world remains disaffected and domestic reconciliation is not forthcoming, it is natural that it would look to co-ethnics elsewhere and to outside powers for support.

Today is the best time to draw or re-draw our political contract in a way that brings the communities together. The Sri Lankan armed forces have reunited the entire territory of the island. The Tamil extremists are weakened to an unprecedented extent by the destruction of their vanguard, the LTTE. They can no longer sustain hardline positions. President Rajapakse has the trust of the Sinhalese to a degree that none of his predecessors had, thanks to his leadership of the liberation war against terrorism and separatism. He can therefore carry the Sinhalese with him into a settlement of the underlying and pre-existing issues. Thus this is the best time for a moderate compromise.

We shall need to pay heed to the views of our friends, local and foreign, as it becomes increasingly obvious that the Tiger army is destroyed but the Tiger movement or global network is still alive, a well-placed new generation of Tamil secessionists have been born overseas and have come of age, and though the war is decisively won, the protracted struggle with Tamil Tiger separatism on a world scale is hardly over. A long cold war may have just begun.

Chapter 8

India, Pakistan and Bangladesh: "Trilaterlism" in South Asia?

Iftekhar Ahmed Chowdhury

This paper argues that, within the context of South Asia, India, Pakistan and Bangladesh have commonalities and potentials that could be positively developed through a policy of "trilateralism". It would imply an informal process of identifying and categorising divisive issues into separate but not water-tight boxes and addressing them with a view to resolving them. Unlike the South Asian Association for Regional Cooperation (SAARC), it would not avoid disputes but confront them. The idea would be to create a strategic "problem solving" partnership that could complement, and not supplant, the SAARC.

Introduction

In South Asia, there is a great deal that its three largest countries — India, Pakistan and Bangladesh — share. Much more than others in the region, they have had a similar historical experience. Prior to 1947, they constituted a single political entity. As Jaswant Singh's book on Muhammad Ali Jinnah underscores, the debate over it notwithstanding, they had common leaders. Mohandas Karamchand Gandhi, Jinnah, Jawaharlal Nehru and Sheikh Mujibur Rahman were all united in their aspiration to free India of British domination. Their efforts eventually found fruition in the emergence of three separate independent and sovereign states, which is an established historical fact. Their pluralist values make them three of the world's largest democracies, with a combined population of nearly 1.5 billion.

Unfortunately, certain colonial legacies fed conflict into their intra-mural relationship. It is a paradox that these countries are known to the world not for their amity, but for the animosities among them.

However, this situation need not be constant. It is an eternal law of nature that everything is in motion. One never steps into the same Indus or the Ganges twice, as those rivers are in constant flux. The flow of history is no different. How can it then be channelled in a way that we move forward, inexorably even if meandering, from conflict to harmony? It will call for a modicum of ingenuity, indeed thinking out of the box, which undoubtedly the peoples and the leadership of the three countries are capable of. As the entire world acknowledges, their intellectual resources are their source of pride. They must be able to muster and press these into their service at a time when they need them more than ever to make that quantum leap from poverty to progress, from protests over each other's behaviour to peace among themselves.

In the recent past, all three countries have experienced successful elections. New governments have emerged in Pakistan and Bangladesh. In India, the electorate returned the same party into power but in a strengthened "avatar". Newness accords impetus to the will to change. The challenge is always to make this change better and more desirable. This should also be the case even if it were to involve a break with the past. The three capitals, and new leaderships, including the one renewed in India, should perhaps focus on this phenomenon. In this they are certain to have the support of their peoples, important for democracies (which all of them are), who are exhausted from decades of strife. In this they will also receive support from the rest of the world.

India–Pakistan Relations

There are positive signals emerging from India and Pakistan in this regard. The relationship between the two powerful nuclear states is key to this desired stability. Pakistan's owning up to a number of its citizens' responsibility for mayhem in Mumbai was a welcome departure from the traditional behaviour pattern of the past. Indeed, it offered the scope to turn a tragedy into an opportunity, and to the credit of both sides, they were able to seize upon it.

It is a good thing too that in all these cases the initiatives made soft beginnings during the period of the immediate past governments. Nothing buttresses the new as an element of continuity, which lends the change a greater degree of robustness.

In the case of India and Pakistan, there was the Pervez Musharraf–Manmohan Singh agreement to strive for a "final settlement" on the Kashmir issue, and not to "allow terrorism to impede the peace process".

These, together with the bus links, the proposed pipelines to carry Iranian and Central Asian oil and gas to India and Pakistan and the reactivation of the Joint Economic Commission, have led both countries to describe their growing understanding as "irreversible". Some recent pronouncements by President Asif Ali Zardari and the Singh-Syed Yousaf Raza Gilani talks in Sharm el-Sheikh have taken the process forward. Given the nature of their past relationship, even a rhetorical advance on some of these highly sensitive subjects can be considered "progress".

India–Bangladesh Relations

Similarly, in terms of India–Bangladesh ties, during the period of the caretaker government in Bangladesh, some hot bilateral issues were brought to the discussion table and the "apolitical" nature of the Bangladesh government allowed for a functionalist approach to some of these subjects, such as water-sharing, transit and connectivity, and the alleged provision of a "safe haven" to Indian insurgents in Bangladeshi territory. The many meetings held between them led both sides to declare that the relationship was on an "irreversible trajectory".

India was not unhappy when power was transferred through elections to an Awami League-led government in January 2009, a party known to be better understood in New Delhi. The then Indian Foreign Minister, Pranab Mukherjee, was the first high-ranking foreign official to visit the new government in February 2009. The stage is now fully set for a visit to India by Prime Minister Sheikh Hasina, in the course of which it has already been stated that the Indian side will not raise issues that might embarrass her.

Pakistan–Bangladesh Relations

The Pakistan–Bangladesh relationship is in some ways less challenging. The two countries share no borders and therefore have no such issues that usually tend to bedevil relations between neighbours in postcolonial settings such as undemarcated boundaries or the sharing of river waters. Being Muslim-majority countries, both, of course, share many common values.

However, while Pakistan is battling terrorism and fundamentalism, Bangladesh is quite happy to maintain and underscore a distinctiveness that allows it to tackle such problems, far less menacing in that country to start with, through poverty alleviation and women empowerment. Thus far, the great value each saw in the other was the possibility of a linkage that could develop into a counterpoise vis-à-vis India, but as their relationships with India improve, this will require replacement by more positive features.

Developing "Trilateralism"

As this set of relationship evolves, India will need to play a critical role. Because of its size, power, influence and endowments, it has to bear a disproportionate responsibility, even if, at times, it is to be without immediate reciprocation. As I have said elsewhere,[1] it should be the "elder" and not the "big" brother; not only the largest country in the heart of South Asia, but the country with the largest heart.

In terms of politics and economics, India, like China, is a country on the rise in the global scene. It seeks not just regional preeminence but also the recognition of a wider international role that it feels it deserves. This can come more easily with the endorsement of its

---

[1] "Post-election India: How the Neighbours View the Elephant", ISAS Insights No. 68, 22 May 2009 (http://www.isasnus.org./events/insights/69.pdf).

neighbours. Thus, how best can the three countries go about developing this "trilateralism" such that they will find it rewarding both individually and collectively?

First, they should perhaps work out a "matrix" detailing the problematic aspects of their relations with a view to solving them. This could involve dividing bilateral issues into categories: those that can be resolved with a bit of effort or "green-box" issues; those that will require some dedicated effort or "orange-box" issues; and those whose resolution for now will be difficult or "red-box" issues. The "lower hanging fruits" of the "green box" may be focussed on at the outset, graduating thereafter to the "orange" and "red" boxes, in the hope that the resultant generation of goodwill from forward movement in one box will positively impact the others.

Second, an informal "strategic partnership" could be evolved between them. It is distinguishable from the more formal "classical alliance". From a theoretical perspective, there are three main ways in which a "strategic partnership" and the more formal "classical alliance" are different. First, a strategic partnership seeks to increase the "power" (which the political philosopher Raymond Aron described as "the capacity of a political unit to impose its will upon other units") of the states involved. A classical alliance may on the other hand be security-oriented (NATO, Warsaw Pact, CENTO, SEATO) or aim at political or economic integration (such as the EU). Second, a strategic partnership is not directed against any common rival but instead has for its goal a general accretion of influence, whereas a classical alliance seeks to balance power against a perceived adversary. And third, a strategic partnership is based upon the mutual objective of increasing individual space of independence, thus allowing for the preservation of national sovereignty whereas alliances through security pacts and political integration tend to sacrifice an element of national defence, or monetary or fiscal policies.

This is exactly why this "trilateralism" and strategic partnership is more likely to succeed in forging a political *entente* than SAARC. The latter is a formal body in which the fear of any erosion of sovereignty precludes political discussions of a serious nature. Moreover, the agreed structure rules out bilateral issues from the agenda, which leads to a "Catch-22" situation. This is because as long as the problems characterise mutual political relations, progress on even functional areas can be rendered difficult. "Trilateralism" will turn this on its head and seek ultimately, and I stress "ultimately", given the recognised complexity of some of these issues, to identify the problems first with a view to resolving them. Nonetheless, the purpose of this "trilateralism" would not be to supplant the more formal SAARC process. Indeed, it should complement and help strengthen it.

The process could begin with a summit of the leaders of India, Pakistan and Bangladesh. In this way, it would be different from what was followed in the case of SAARC. In the latter case it began with meetings at official levels, from Foreign Secretaries working their way through the Ministers, to a summit of the leaders. By the time the Heads of Government got round to their first conference, too many bureaucratic hurdles were already created, tending to restrain them. In the present case, it could be initiated with a summit of the leaders of the three countries, even in an informal "retreat" mode, providing them maximum leeway to decide how to proceed. If it succeeds, it would radically alter the course, not just of regional but of international relations.

It is not necessary to resolve all or even some of the problems. However, the mere demonstration of a will to do so, with a structure put in place (the "boxes"), will make a huge difference. This will not only facilitate the rise of India, but will also enable Pakistan and Bangladesh to follow in a "flying geese" formation, to the benefit of all their peoples. Surely this is an idea that must not take long in materialising! It will require a change in mindsets. That implies that the vast population of these three countries has a hill to climb. Waiting will not make it any smaller.

Index

List of Contributors

Mr K Shanmugam is Minister for Home Affairs and Minister for Law, Republic of Singapore.

Dr Amitendu Palit is Head (Development & Programmes) and Visiting Senior Research Fellow at the Institute of South Asian Studies (ISAS), National University of Singapore (NUS).

Professor Dilip M. Nachane is Senior Professor, Indira Gandhi Institute of Development Research (IGIDR), India and Honorary Senior Fellow, ISAS, NUS.

Mr Mani Shankar Aiyar is Member of Parliament, India, and former Minister for Petroleum & Natural Gas, former Minister of Panchayati Raj and former Minister for Youth Affairs and Sports, India.

Mr Sartaj Aziz is Vice Chancellor of Beaconhouse National University in Lahore, Pakistan and former Finance Minister and Foreign Minister of Pakistan.

Professor T.V. Paul is James McGill Professor of International Relations & Director, Centre for International Peace and Security Studies (CIPSS), McGill University, Canada.

Professor Rasul Bakhsh Rais is Professor, School of Humanities, Social Sciences & Law, Department of Humanities and Social Sciences, Lahore University of Management Sciences (LUMS), Pakistan.

Dr Dayan Jayatilleka is Ambassador Designate, Embassy of Sri Lanka, France and Honorary Senior Fellow, ISAS, NUS.

Dr Iftekhar Ahmed Chowdhury is Senior Research Fellow at ISAS, NUS and former Foreign Adviser (Foreign Minister) of Bangladesh.